The Quantum University

The Quantum University

New Knowledge Requires New Thinking

Perry R. Rettig

ROWMAN & LITTLEFIELD
Lanham • Boulder • New York • London

Published by Rowman & Littlefield
An imprint of The Rowman & Littlefield Publishing Group, Inc.
4501 Forbes Boulevard, Suite 200, Lanham, Maryland 20706
www.rowman.com

6 Tinworth Street, London SE11 5AL, United Kingdom

Copyright © 2021 by Perry R. Rettig

All rights reserved. No part of this book may be reproduced in any form or by any electronic or mechanical means, including information storage and retrieval systems, without written permission from the publisher, except by a reviewer who may quote passages in a review.

British Library Cataloguing in Publication Information Available

Library of Congress Cataloging-in-Publication Data

Names: Rettig, Perry Richard, author.
Title: The quantum university : new knowledge requires new thinking / Perry R. Rettig.
Description: Lanham, Maryland : Rowman & Littlefield, 2021. | Includes bibliographical references. | Summary: "American universities were not designed to be nimble and responsive to the changes necessary to meet today's challenges. The Quantum University describes lessons learned from the contemporary sciences which can then serve as guideposts to help our university leaders meet these challenges" — Provided by publisher.
Identifiers: LCCN 2020046547 (print) | LCCN 2020046548 (ebook) | ISBN 9781475859133 (cloth) | ISBN 9781475859140 (paper) | ISBN 9781475859157 (epub)
Subjects: LCSH: Education, Higher—United States—Administration | Universities and colleges—United States—Administration. | Education, Higher—Aims and objectives—United States. | Educational change—United States.
Classification: LCC LB2341 .R4758 2021 (print) | LCC LB2341 (ebook) | DDC 378.1/01—dc23
LC record available at https://lccn.loc.gov/2020046547
LC ebook record available at https://lccn.loc.gov/2020046548

Dedication

The Quantum University *is dedicated to my four grandsons: Adrian, Jeremiah, Theo, and Oliver. You inspire me to struggle for a better future for you. May a spirit of connection and creativity drive you in whatever endeavors you pursue in this life.*
The Quantum University *is also dedicated to our leaders. It is not intended for our managers nor those interested in maintaining the status quo. We need leaders to step up with a creative spirit, one that welcomes a bit of chaos, creates a place for inspiration, and strives to embrace the human dynamic within our organizations.*

Contents

List of Table and Figures	ix
Preface	xi
Acknowledgments	xv
Introduction	1
1 Old School	9
2 You've Got a New Thing Coming	27
3 A Butterfly Spreads Her Wings	49
4 Quantum Redux	73
5 The Quantum University—Thought Experiment	95
Bibliography	121
About the Author	127

List of Table and Figures

TABLE

Table 1.1 Professional-Bureaucratic Matrix   15

FIGURES

Figure 2.1 Double-Slit Experiment   32
Figure 3.1 Ecological Pyramid Model   50
Figure 3.2 Higher Education Organizational Pyramid Model   50
Figure 3.3 Ecological Pyramid Model with Checks & Balances   52
Figure 3.4 Higher Education Organizational Pyramid Model
            with Checks & Balances   53
Figure 3.5 Glycerin Experiment   54
Figure 3.6 Dissipative Structure—Benard Cells   59
Figure 4.1 Dimensionality   76
Figure 4.2 Birth of a New Universe from a Black Hole   80
Figure 4.3 Maslow's Hierarchy of Needs   81
Figure 5.1 Dolan's Governance Pyramid Model   107
Figure 5.2 Shared Governance Involvement for Boards of
            Advisers, Staff Council, Student Government
            Association, and with a Process for Checks & Balances   108

Preface

"The truth is that we are, in fact, talking about a revolution."[1]

—Peter Block

American colleges and universities, both public and private, are experiencing an environmental shift like none they have seen in decades.[2] WICHE (Western Interstate Commission for Higher Education) data indicates that an enrollment crisis has already hit the Northeast and Midwest regions of our nation, while the other regions will see significant enrollment declines by the middle of the decade.[3] Revenue streams continue to dry up, public support continues to diminish; the result is an increase in college closures.[4] The old model isn't working, but it never did.

A cursory glance at declining high school enrollments might suggest difficult but manageable losses for institutions of higher learning. However, a deeper analysis indicates much more dire problems. Traditional white college-attending populations are showing double-digit declines. Any potentially mitigating differences are made up by near-term growth in underrepresented populations. These populations, however, earn 60 percent total family income of their majority counterparts,[5] and are typically less prepared for college. By the end of the decade, even these populations show a precipitous drop. The reason? With the economic crisis in 2008–2009, families had fewer children.

This book is premised on the understanding that current organizational models are not suited to be able to address these and other emerging crises. To the contrary, they are built on purpose to maintain the status quo and therefore not able to adapt to change. The resulting hegemony has debilitated sound decision-making and lost efficacy along the way. The model we use to govern our institutions has been formulated on science—the classical sciences of Newtonian physics. While the science is sound, its application is wholly misplaced for running dynamic, human organizations. The machine metaphor does not fit—it never did!

American universities have not evolved along with the contemporary sciences they teach in their lecture halls. If we are to use science to help us frame our organizational structures and governance models—to make them contemporary and nimble in order to meet ever-changing demands—we need to look to quantum physics, to the current lessons from ecology, and to the other newer sciences. The metaphor shifts from clockworks to nature. Frederick Taylor and Douglas McGregor described and studied classical organizational structures based on these classical sciences. Now, a new generation of leaders and scholars need to create and study new organizational structures and models based upon these emerging sciences.

Again, Newtonian or classical physics is a sound and credible science, but its application to our organizations is inappropriate. This science that spurred on the Industrial Revolution is not the science to serve as the basis for our leadership and governance models. The traditional view is more rational, linear and simple, whereas the new view is more intuitive, multifaceted, and complex. The past view is more reductionistic and encourages competition, while the newer thinking is more holistic and encourages cooperation.

Mathematics is the language of the sciences. Classical physics uses the quantitative mathematics of linear algebra, analytic geometry, and calculus. Quantum physics also uses the qualitative mathematics of dynamic systems theory, topology geometry, and fractal geometry. In other words, the new sciences use the mathematics of relationships and patterns.[6]

In *Nature Loves to Hide,* Shimon Malin explained, "Newtonian physics is based entirely on sensory evidence. Its spectacular success led scientists to consider other types of experiences, such as feelings or intuitions, irrelevant. . . . But what if Plato and Plotinus are right? What if deep truths become available precisely when one finds a way to leave sensory experiences behind and transcend the subject/object mode of perception?"[7]

Ilya Prigogine and Isabelle Stengers wrote, "Our vision of nature is undergoing a radical change toward the multiple, the temporal, and complex."[8] In terms of new leadership, Kotter recognized, "When managers today produce successful change in organizations . . . the process is time consuming and highly complex."[9] In other words, the model must fit the context. The good news is the new science is already there providing us a map forward. This book will lay out the key principles of these new sciences and then explore the implications and applications for our emergent organizational structure and our leadership.

*"To see a World in a Grain of Sand, and a Heaven in a Wild Flower,
Hold Infinity in the palm of your hand, and Eternity in an hour."*

William Blake: "Auguries of Innocence"

NOTES

1. Peter Block, *Stewardship: Choosing Service over Self-Interest* (San Francisco: Berrett-Koehler, 1996), 44.

2. Jeffrey Docking, *Crisis in Higher Education: A Plan to Save Small Liberal Arts Colleges in America* (East Lansing, MI: Michigan State University Press, 2015).

3. WICHE: Western Interstate Commission for Higher Education (*Knocking at the College Door* 2016).

Additional and supporting data can be found at: U.S. Department of Education, Institute of Education Sciences, National Center for Education Statistics (*Digest of Education Statistics*, 2017).

4. Robert Zemsky, Susan Shaman, and Susan Campbell Baldridge, *The College Stress Test: Tracking Institutional Futures Across a Crowded Market* (Baltimore, MD: Johns Hopkins University Press, 2020).

5. College Board, *Trends in College Pricing* www.collegeboard.org. 2018.

President of Albion College (MI) foretold these concerns: "Economic insecurity throughout the country compounds enrollment problems at many small private colleges because parents and students believe students won't find jobs that will enable them to pay off college debt" Jeffrey Docking, 2015, 9.

6. Perry Rettig, *Quantum Leaps in School Leadership* (Lanham, MD: Rowman & Littlefield, 2002), x.

7. Shimon Malin, *Nature Loves to Hide: Quantum Physics and the Nature of Reality, a Western Perspective* (Oxford, United Kingdom: Oxford University Press, 2001), 238.

8. Ilya Prigogine and Isabelle Stengers, *Order out of Chaos* (New York: Bantam Books, 1984), 2.

9. John Kotter, *What Leaders Really Do* (Cambridge, MA: Harvard Business School Press, 1999), ix.

Acknowledgments

A project such as *The Quantum University* requires the collaboration of numerous hard-working and dedicated professionals. I need to acknowledge several of those individuals who made this book become a reality. First, those four individuals who wrote pragmatic essays directly from the field have driven home the key concepts espoused throughout this book. Martin Tadlock, Jaime Hunt, Joe Dennis, and Rinardo Reddick are those professionals who grounded these notions with a sense of reality.

Further, Cat Wiles labored through the tedious tasks of preparing charts, tables, and graphs for this project. Her hours of dedication show in this body of work. Felicia Lively-Tucker and Kim Hartman reviewed a late draft of this manuscript and provided the feedback necessary to drive the project to conclusion. Finally, I have deep gratitude for the publisher and editors at Rowman & Littlefield for their support of such independent thinking and to give voice which at times may be out of the mainstream. It is from this support and these efforts that creativity and new ways of thinking can take root.

I am grateful to each of these professionals and for the countless colleagues who support them every day.

Introduction

"The largely unconscious embrace of the mechanistic approach to management has now become one of the main obstacles to organizational change."[1]

Higher education leaders are not the only ones required to make change. Book publishers, for example, were facing an existential crisis as digital print emerged. People bought many fewer traditional books, and publishers needed to change in order to survive. The market has found a new norm, and people are still purchasing traditional books, but fewer than before. Shifting to e-books saved the industry.[2] The publishing industry changed and is thriving in a new normal. Just as traditional book publishers needed to change to their environment, college leaders must make structural changes in order to survive in the new market. While the market continues to change, those institutions that adapt will exist and thrive in the decades to come. This book is intended for those brave individuals who seek to change their institutions of higher learning. This audience includes members of boards of trustees, senior campus leadership, students of higher education, and faculty leaders—all those who are entrusted and empowered to make change.

Fortunately, we have been provided some guideposts to help our imagination. In *The Tao of Physics*, Fritjof Capra wrote, "The fundamental change of worldview that is occurring in science and in society . . . a change that is nothing less than the unfolding of a new vision of reality—and the social implications of this cultural transformation for the centuries to come."[3]

Each chapter of this book focuses on a primary theme, that of a new science, as well as subsequent lessons for organizational structure and governance, leadership, and implications and applications for our leaders. In addition, each chapter includes a story of Leslie O'Connor, who will be introduced shortly. Ms. O'Connor is a new trustee at Southbey University and is quickly disillusioned by her experience in what feels to her as merely serving as a figurehead institutional leader with no real sense of efficacy. Finally, essays from practitioner experts in the field conclude each chapter. These authors share their insights as they have grappled with topics covered herein.

Chapter 1 serves as a descriptor of the classical Newtonian model for organizational structure and leadership. It describes the fallacious presuppositions upon which the model is based and then describes why the model is an inappropriate metaphor for our institutions—especially to be adaptive to address the necessary shifts in our contemporary environment.

This chapter will conclude by following Leslie O'Connor's frustrations as a new board of trustee member and her growing sense of losing efficacy in her leadership role. Jaime Hunt will conclude this chapter with an essay which provides an experiential analysis of why current models of leadership don't work but how a new relational model does work. Hunt is vice president and chief communications and marketing officer at Miami of Ohio.

Chapter 2 immediately delves into the theories of relativity and quantum physics. These sciences will be explicated with a sense and sensibility for the lay reader. The first half of the chapter will conclude by discussing a new metaphor and why these sciences provide a better model for organizing and leading today's institutions of higher learning.

The latter half of chapter 2 will continue with Leslie O'Connor. She will begin to wrestle with imagining a new way to lead; she will, through a cloudy mist, envision a new role for herself and a new way to lead. This story will be followed by an essay penned by Rinardo Reddick who will provide an essay depicting tough lessons learned from the field that might provide pragmatic direction for our institutional leaders. Dr. Reddick is the chief diversity officer of Westchester Community College in New York.

Chapter 3 is devoted to a description of the newer ecological sciences; chaos theory; the science of complexity; and dissipative structures. Just as in chapter 2, this chapter will provide new insights for application in creating new organizational structures and models of leadership for colleges to be ever nimble to changing demands.

Leslie will continue her internal dialogue about what is and maybe what could be. She will turn to mentors, both past and new, for their insights as well as to bounce off her emerging ideas. Dr. Joe Dennis will provide an extant lay of the land in higher education describing different leadership models with their associated strengths and weaknesses. He will describe his own experiences from the field of each approach. Dr. Dennis serves as the department chair and professor of Mass Communications at Piedmont College in Georgia.

Chapter 4 revisits quantum physics through a contemporary lens of new understandings by briefly revisiting the work of Albert Einstein then leaping to the quantum brain, holographs, the big bang, black holes, and multiple universes. Lessons learned from these sciences will be stipulated in succinct fashion.

Leslie sees other types of boards at work and begins to imagine a new role for her college board of trustees and perhaps a board of advisors. Her best friend, LaShonda, exemplifies a new way of entrepreneurial thinking. Dr. Martin Tadlock will author the final essay of this book and will span the final two chapters. He will express insights and experiences about change in our organizations through the lens of Critical Theory and with thoughts about what the future might be. Dr. Tadlock is the regional chancellor at the University of South Florida, St. Petersburg.

Chapter 5 pulls everything together. It makes the implicit lessons learned in the previous chapters more explicit. In other words, it goes beyond general principles of a new way of thinking about our leadership and how we organize our institutions to describing what our new leadership practices will be and how our organizations will look. It gets pragmatic, and we'll see that these changes already have a model and can be instituted with some grit and realism.

This book will conclude with finding Leslie assuming a new leadership role. We will see her trying out her ideas through the good, the bad, and the ugly. Her ride will be bumpy, but she will find inspiration in places she never expected. The second half of Dr. Martin Tadlock's essay will conclude here with a focus of what could be.

Let us conclude here with these prophetic words from Fritjof Capra and Pier Luigi Luisi:

> As the twenty-first century unfolds, it is becoming more and more evident that the major problems of our time . . . cannot be understood in isolation. They are systemic problems, which means that they are all interconnected and interdependent. . . . Unfortunately, this realization has not yet dawned on most of our political leaders, who are unable to "connect the dots," to use a popular phrase.[4]

LESLIE'S LAMENT

Leslie was about to begin her first year of a three-year term on the Southbey University Board of Trustees. She knew it wasn't her career as an English teacher that brought her invitation to serve on the board; rather, it was her family inheritance. After all, her parents were on the ground floor of the Artificial

Intelligence industry boom. Whatever the reason for her position on the board, Leslie was determined to be active and get her family's money's worth.

From the outset, she had an underlying sense of uneasiness. She heard the board came together three times a year and were otherwise quiescent throughout the year. Board meetings were perfunctory for the most part; the university president and his cabinet put on a glossy and impressive program, and the trustee executive committee controlled the discussion. Everything was clean, professional, and tidy. But, no serious debate or dialogue ensued. If an attempt was made, it was quickly eschewed or rebuffed by members of the powerful executive committee.

To be honest, she was about to learn, these meetings were actually quite impressive. As a matter of fact, the indoctrination began before the first meeting. Two weeks prior to the first session, she received a manual from the university president, Dr. Samuel P. Leonard. The manual outlined: the university's history, board responsibilities, ethics and conflict of interest policies, policy manual for the campus, and board committee duties. She was also given a link taking her to the agenda for the upcoming board meeting. The agenda had tabs and sub-tabs containing supporting documents in excess of 300 pages. She had her work cut out for her. She was also expected to give a personal contribution—a minimum of $5,000 to the university annual fund. This expectation of all board members seemed rather unfair to her as she was living off her teacher salary.

Leslie was appointed to the Student Affairs Committee. So, while she tried to prepare by reading all the board reports, she gave most of her focus to this committee's agenda and support documents. She wanted to be prepared for her first meeting, and she had so many questions; she felt rather embarrassed. But, truly, some of this seemed so ridiculous. All these crazy acronyms and strange vocabularies: FTE, FTIC, EFC, Yield, Melt, Persistence, just to name a few.

Tons of data tables were shared with indicating green and yellow arrows. Things certainly looked good through a quantitative lens, but what about quality? What was the college-experience like for the students? Were they being successful once they left? Leslie wanted to know more than graduation rates, rates of job placement, and rates of grad school placement. How long did it take for them to pay off their student loans? Were they being successful in their careers and in their communities?

As the first meeting arrived, Leslie entered the meeting with a strong sense of anxiety, enthusiasm, and anticipation. She was greeted by new colleagues: fellow trustees, senior administrators, and staff. Leslie kind of felt like royalty. A breakfast array awaited all trustees as they entered their committee rooms. This certainly felt quite professional, and an eagerness to begin was palpable for everyone in the room.

Committee chair, Fiona Avery, called the meeting to order. As the trustee chair of the Student Affairs Committee, she was prepared by offering welcoming remarks and a topical coverage of the morning's agenda. She then turned the dais over to vice president for Student Affairs and Enrollment Management Gino Beronnelli. Dr. Beronnelli seemed both intelligent and rather slick. He knew his field and had a presence about him. Committee members listened. The agenda started with a presentation covering enrollment data—current and predictions. The vice president was matter-of-fact in his Power Point presentation and seemed quite positive. Along the back wall sat his dean and associate dean of Enrollment Management. They were in attendance to answer any questions. There were some comments and questions after the presentation, but all seemed perfunctory to Leslie.

This presentation was followed by the enthusiastic and mercurial athletic director Allen Binkowski. Winning records, athlete GPAs, awards, and commendations were the focus. This was all received with great enthusiasm amid fun discussion. Preliminary discussion of a new football practice facility and training complex held the greatest time of the dialogue. The Finance Committee would be handling the funding planning.

The next forty-five minutes were given back to Dr. Bertonnelli as he covered the broad ranging division of Student Affairs. He presented another PowerPoint highlighting Residence Halls, Student Activities, and Student Support Services including Financial Aid, Counseling, Tutoring, and Career Services. Directors from each of these units sat dutifully along the side of the room. They, too, were there to provide additional information and to answer questions. Leslie's fellow board members were quite engaged in this portion of the presentation, and she asked her first question: "Do you do some sort of student satisfaction survey and any sort of alumni surveys, Dr. Bertonnelli?"

"Absolutely, Ms. O'Connor," came Dr. Beronnelli's response. "As a matter of fact, we will be giving our annual student satisfactory inventory in early March and our alumni survey this summer. I'll speak more about both of these at our spring board meetings." That was it; end of conversation.

Leslie thought to herself, "Perhaps the fall meeting would be the appropriate place to discuss these survey results." She didn't say these thoughts aloud, though.

The final twenty minutes of the morning committee meeting was devoted to a short presentation by two senior students. Peter was a lacrosse athlete. He spoke of his four years at Southbey, how he was a shy poorly prepared freshman but grew into the all-conference captain of the team. He looked back with fond memories and talked of his present internship with a local marketing firm.

Heather spoke of her experiences as a nontraditional student raising a family of four, working part-time, and ultimately finding great success both in the classroom and as a Student Government Association leader. She had a remarkable story of success at Southbey, due in large part to the extensive student support services on campus and the online course offerings. Heather would graduate in December, and already had a job offer as a paralegal in the state capital.

This short presentation by the students garnered the greatest excitement from the committee members. It was acknowledged by all that they wished they had more time with the students, but wished them well in their careers ahead, and thanked them for their time and for choosing Southbey.

Leslie and her fellow trustee committee members were escorted by Dr. Bertonnelli and the other administrators to join all the other committees for lunch at the Student Commons. It was a very pleasant and celebratory event. A splendid buffet was provided, followed by the president's welcoming remarks and a presentation by two recent graduates who spoke about how their experiences at Southbey prepared them for their new careers. After this 75-minute lunch event, all trustees and senior leadership team members headed to the board room for the afternoon full board meeting.

The atmosphere remained collegial, but there was clearly a different aura; it was very business-like, punctual, and formal. Committee reports were direct and succinct. Motions made and votes affirmed. Very little discussion took place. Leslie got the feeling any real discussion took place at the committee level. The full board was more pro forma. With all the formal committee presentations, the afternoon flew by and was concluded by 5:00 p.m. Some of the trustees headed out together for dinner—plans had already been made. Leslie headed home. Well, she headed to her high school freshman daughter's volleyball game.

Sitting on the rickety wooden gymnasium bleachers, Leslie reflected on the day. She realized that quickly and quietly she was enculturated about her role in the governance of the university and who was in charge. "Were all university boards like this?" Leslie questioned herself. To understand the workings of the university was truly overwhelming. She didn't know what she didn't know. "What value do I bring to this board?"

NOTES

1. Fritjof Capra and Pier Luigi Luisi, *The Systems View of Life: A Unifying Vision* (Cambridge, United Kingdom: Cambridge University Press, 2014), 59.

2. Lynn Neary, "Morning Edition: Interview on Book Publishing," *National Public Radio* (November 26, 2019).

> Porter-O'Grady and Malloch have also looked at the new sciences as models for change in the health care industry. See: Tim Porter-O'Grady and Kathy Malloch, *Quantum*

Leadership: Creating Sustainable Value in Health Care (Burlington, MA: Jones and Bartlett, 2017).

3. Fritjof Capra, *The Tao of Physics: An Exploration of the Parallels between Modern Physics and Eastern Mysticism* (Boston: Shambhala, 2000), 6.

Capra went further by quoting eminent physicist Werner Heisenberg: "It is probably true quite generally that in the history of human thinking the most fruitful developments frequently take place at those points where two different lines of thought meet . . . one may hope that new and interesting developments may follow" (4).

4. Fritjof Capra and Pier Luigi Luisi, *The Systems View of Life: A Unifying Vision* (Cambridge, United Kingdom: Cambridge University Press, 2014), xi.

Chapter 1

Old School

"Today's [classical thinking] systems of concepts contain deep seated incongruities."

"In spite of the fact that, today, we know positively that classical mechanics fails as a foundation dominating all physics, it still occupies the center of all our thinking in physics."[1]

—Albert Einstein (1936)

It seems fitting to begin this book with two quotes written in an essay by Albert Einstein. Einstein soared passed classical physics, via his thought experiments, to a new understanding of the universe, yet he struggled with the direction his latter contemporaries were leading. His theories of relativity were the necessary advancement that made quantum physics possible. However, the basis for our current models of organizational structure and our management practices predate Einstein and subsequent quantum theorists. In fact, these models originated in the era of Sir Isaac Newton, yet they remain ensconced in our organizations to this day.

These traditional or classical models expect a great deal of control and authority by those individuals we place in leadership positions.[2] Newtonian physics has helped man to understand the movement of the planets in our solar system and of the stars in the heavens. It has helped man create machines that operate with expected and planned efficiency. It has provided man with comforts and luxuries that have helped to make life more livable and even enjoyable.

This has been a good science for so much of what we need and use today. It has helped to create an existence of mechanistic simplicity and predictability. But the application of the science is flawed when it comes to understanding the lives of people and of the phenomenon of work environments. Newtonian science is linear and is perhaps sufficient for the understanding of machines but not for the understanding of the complexities of humans and their social organizations. Let us take a brief review of this archetypal science.

Classical physics provided the opportunity for scientists to better understand *things*. As the science explicitly suggests, if you can just break down the complex whole and study its parts individually, you can understand the whole and make predictions about its future. You can then provide an algorithm for success and for replication.

This philosophy might work for machines and planetary movements, but it cannot do justice to understanding the complexities and dynamics of people and of the organizations within which they work. This traditional approach is appropriate for its area of study—closed, mechanical systems. Unfortunately, theorists and practitioners in other fields have taken its fundamental principles and applied them erroneously to fields that don't fit the model.

Behaviorists like John Watson and B.F. Skinner applied this Newtonian mechanistic linear prediction to the study of human life and behavior. "Economists, philosophers, and political theorists soon grafted Newton's natural law onto all aspects of life."[3] To reiterate, the science is inappropriate here. Physics professor at the University of California Berkeley Henry Stapp posited:

> The behaviorists sought to explain human behavior in terms of certain relatively simple mechanisms, such as stimulus and response, habit formation, habit integration, and conditioning of various kinds. It is now generally agreed that the simple mechanisms identified by the behaviorists cannot adequately account for the full complexity of human behavior.[4]

Frederick Taylor then applied this same behavioral method to understanding how to make employees work more efficiently and how to provide the management in order to control the desired results. (More on Taylor's work later in this chapter.) Stephen Covey, however, explained his concern with this line of reasoning. "You simply can't think *efficiency* with people. You think *effectiveness* with *people* and *efficiency* with *things*."[5]

The flaw lies in the belief that people can be dissected and understood and controlled like machines. It believes that leaders must motivate and think for the workers. It believes that work must be broken down into ever smaller parts in order to understand the whole. It does not take into account the human equation. It does not take into account how the parts affect the whole in interconnected ways that cannot be measured in isolation. It does not take into account the incomprehensible interconnectedness of the relationships within the whole. Margaret Wheatley, a former professor of management at

Brigham Young University and a leading thinker in the new sciences, perhaps summarizes this discussion best:

> Each of us lives and works in organizations designed from Newtonian images of the universe. We manage by separating things into parts, we believe that influence occurs as a direct result of force exerted from one person to another, we engage in complex planning for a world that we keep expecting to be predictable, and we search continually for better methods of objectively perceiving the world. . . . [These assumptions] are the base from which we design and manage organizations.[6]

In order to see why this traditional approach to leadership based upon classical physics is inappropriate, it is necessary to understand the physics. The following section will briefly describe the key principles of classical *physics*, which will be followed by a brief description of the key principles of classical *leadership*.

KEY PRINCIPLES OF CLASSICAL PHYSICS

Classical physics starts with the premise that objectivity leads to predictability. In order to make predictions, the researcher must be completely objective; there must be a separation of the subject and the object. In other words, the observer must not be part of the experiment—they must look in from the outside. This science leads to a reductionist, deterministic mindset with a clock works metaphor. It has led to our contemporary models of organization and leadership. Unfortunately, this model is inappropriate beyond its limited uses. As systems thinker Peter Senge put it:

> From a very early age, we are taught to break apart problems, to fragment the world. This apparently makes complex tasks and subjects more manageable, but we pay a hidden, enormous price. We can no longer see the consequences of our actions; we lose our intrinsic sense of connection to the larger whole.[7]

It is quite apparent that classical physics is founded on linear, mechanistic thinking. The foundation of this science is a study of the parts in a reductionistic fashion in order to understand the whole. Each component is separated from the whole, studied in detail, and put back together. For the purposes here, the key principles of classical sciences are:

(1) Objectivity
(2) Reductionism

(3) Linear/Deterministic
(4) Control
(5) Replication
(6) Prediction

Just how do these principles of Newtonian physics impact our notions of leadership? The following section will describe the concepts from classical physics that administrators have borrowed to create traditional models of management.

KEY PRINCIPLES OF CLASSICAL LEADERSHIP

It must be made clear that there is no explicit Newtonian model of leadership; however, it is this author's assertion that traditional models of leadership have built their foundations upon the principles of classical physics. The inchoate management model of classical organizational thought, also referred to as scientific management, emerged from the classical sciences. Just a few examples include the modern assembly line;[8] political, corporate, and military power structures;[9] Keynesian economics;[10] the conventional study of biology;[11] strategic planning;[12] professional journalism;[13] and, the behavioral study in psychology.[14]

The classical sciences provide the framework for the scientific study of organizations; Frederick Taylor provided the scholarship. An American with an engineering background, Taylor believed that organizations could be studied and rationally understood. His time and motion studies were conducted in order to organize each type of work so that time and effort were minimized. Basic features of this model are well known by all who have studied leadership. Taylor conceptualized four principles of scientific management:

(1) Eliminate the guesswork of rule-of-thumb approaches to decide how each worker is to do a job by adopting scientific measurements to break the job down into a series of small, related tasks.
(2) Use more scientific, systematic methods for selecting workers and training them for specific jobs.
(3) Establish a clear division of responsibility between management and workers, with management doing the goal setting, planning, and supervising and workers executing the required tasks.
(4) Establish the discipline whereby management sets the objectives and the workers cooperate in achieving them.[15]

These principles of scientific management played a central role in the design of administration in this new era.

Large organizations were the by-product of the Industrial Age. The industrial leaders needed ways to understand and manage these monolithic structures. The machines that were created in these factories served as models for the organization of their own industries. Closed Systems thinking was born, and the machine metaphor served as its exemplar. Industrialists thought they could run their manufacturing systems like the machines they made, and in fact, they did manage their organizations in a corresponding fashion.

Closed Systems thinking is all about efficiency and effectiveness. The goal is to maximize productivity. It is a positivistic or deterministic approach that requires linear, rational decision-making. The Newtonian sciences led to Closed Systems thinking and provided the theoretical framework for the development of the industrial model for organizational structure and governance.

French industrialist Henry Fayol had executive-level work experience, and he began the actual study of Classical Organizational Thought. "He advocated that all managers perform five basic functions: planning, organizing, commanding, coordinating, and controlling.[16] Followers of Fayol's work seemed to have missed his concern that administrators use these principles flexibly and that they use judgement in carrying out their responsibilities.

Max Weber—a German sociologist—concerned about the arbitrary power in the hands of the few, formulated bureaucratic structures in order to legitimize authority in the hands of experts. Structurally, Weber believed that all good organizations should share certain characteristics for the purpose of efficiency. First, they all should have a division of labor and specialization. For example, there are various levels and departments, and each unit and position has specific responsibilities.

Second, there should be an impersonal orientation. This allows administrators to make decisions based upon facts, not feelings, and to treat each person equally. Third, all organizations need a hierarchy of authority. This provides for clear patterns of communication and guarantees that workers will carry out their superiors' orders. Fourth, good systems need rules and regulations understood by all employees. This stipulation ensures uniformity and stability of employee work.

Finally, bureaucratic organizations require a career orientation. With this guarantee, quality work is rewarded with employee promotion. While Weber advocated for bureaucratic structures, he was also concerned that bureaucracies could become too strong, and therefore, dangerous. This seems to be yet another lesson lost on many of our contemporary leaders—the proverbial tail that wags the dog. But as higher education organizations got bigger, there was a tendency to create greater differentiation, academic specialization, and bureaucratization.[17]

Organizational guru, Peter Block advanced, "Functional organizations with deep silos, are the ideal structure for command-and-control governance. They were born of the industrial revolution where economies of scale and specialization of labor became the religion. Functional organizations make administration easier."[18]

Critics of the Weberian Model have always existed, but these are more a criticism of bureaucracies and not of Weber's depiction.[19] They point out that such bureaucratization hurts staff morale and causes worker boredom. These same critics decry the fact that communication patterns are not more efficient,[20] that workers have no control of their goals and work environment, and that there is a conflict between achievement and seniority. Charles Heckscher argued, "All of Weber's forms of legitimate authority are essentially structures of domination—that is, contexts in which the higher level can command *without giving a justification.*"[21]

Bureaucratic practices also produce legalism—where frustrated workers follow their job descriptions to the letter, not working to their full potential. Feminists feel that these organizations are gender-biased.[22] And, most interestingly, the Weberian Model assumes that subordinates have less technical expertise than their superiors. This last point is critical to our understanding of today's organizational culture. The hidden assumption is that our professors and professional staff know less than the senior administrators: the model is built with this in mind—that the bosses know more than the professional staff they employee.

Mihaly Csikszentmihalyi warned, "The evidence suggests that the Industrial Revolution not only shortened the life spans of members of several generations, but made them more nasty and brutish as well."[23] Again, Max Weber described bureaucratic structures in order to make organizations more efficient, the work of the workers less ambiguous, and to take the power out of the hands of the few.

But according to Francis X. Neumann Jr., "The Weberian bureaucracy was totally suitable to a Weberian world, for a world of industrial or second wave society, but it may not be altogether appropriate for the new and more complex environments [of today]."[24] Citizens and the workers in these organizations know it and have learned to distrust it causing an apostasy in our institutions.[25]

Organizations can be categorized as to the extent they are influenced by professional and bureaucratic norms. (See table 1.1). Organizations that have a high level of professional norms and standards and have a high degree of bureaucratic structures are considered "Weberian." Clearly, today's typical universities fall into this category and is the model to which most aspire. Conversely, some institutions have high levels of bureaucracy, yet few professional attributes. Much of industrial world falls into this category. These organizations are considered "bureaucratic," of course.

Table 1.1   Professional-Bureaucratic Matrix

		Bureaucracy HIGH	LOW
Professional	HIGH	Weberian	Professional
	LOW	Bureaucratic	Chaotic

Copyright Permission is not necessary

Other institutions have high levels of professionalism with little bureaucratic regulation and oversight. These typically are small institutions originated by professional entrepreneurs. However, as they become more and more successful, they grow. In order to maintain control of the values and vision of the organization, the leaders put bureaucratic structures into place, with a resulting Weberian lean. Such institutions with professional attributes are naturally considered "professional."

Still other institutions have low levels of professional expertise accompanied by low degrees of bureaucratic structure; they are considered "chaotic." Numerous start-up attempts are made and ultimately fail with no special expertise or standard structures as guideposts. No one wants to work in these organizations which founder about adrift searching for a semblance of order. Indeed, it is the Weberian Model to which most organizations ultimately gravitate.

Both democratic and communist worlds have utilized Newtonian processes of control. "Strategic thinking has become the dominant mode of professional action, just as strategic decisions have become central to planning and management in most public and private organizations," according to St. John.[26] In describing Soviet Communist economic control, Francis Fukuyama further stipulated, "Indeed, the speed with which this transformation occurred seemed to demonstrate to many people that centralized planning under a police-state tyranny was in fact a *more* effective means of achieving rapid industrialization than free people operating in free markets,"[27] but with a terrible price and without long-lasting success.

In this classical model, employees knew who the boss was. The boss did the hiring, and the boss did the firing. The model was clean and straightforward. It was the proverbial iron fist. This model was considered a closed system model, as work was able to be controlled from within the organization. Other closed system models followed.

Classical organization management was the model of practice from 1900 to 1930 in the nation. As a reaction to its shortcomings, two other definitive approaches emerged. From 1930 to 1950 the "people-oriented" human relations approach took over as a reaction to classical organizational management's failure to acknowledge the informal organization, the intrinsic motivation of the workers, the dynamics of social systems, and the idiosyncrasies of the individual. The now famous Western Electric Hawthorne Studies showed:

(1) Economic incentives are not the only significant motivators. In fact, non-economic social sanctions limit the effectiveness of economic incentives.
(2) Workers respond to management as members of an informal group, not as individuals.
(3) Production levels are limited more by the social norms of the informal organization than by physiological capacities.
(4) Specialization does not necessarily create the most efficient organization of the work group.
(5) Workers use the informal organization to protect themselves from arbitrary management decisions.
(6) Informal social organizations will interact with management.
(7) A narrow span of control is not a prerequisite to effective supervision.
(8) Informal leaders are often as important as formal supervisors.
(9) Individuals are active human beings, not passive cogs in a machine.[28]

Management expert, Jean Lipman-Bluman, further stated that, "It soon became apparent that the small group—not just management authority—was an important source of workers' commitment and discipline."[29] She went on to explain, "When people participate in the decision making process, they tend to become more committed to the decision and therefore more likely willing to implement it."[30]

Many organizational management experts felt that the human relations approach, on the other hand, did not provide accountability and was too laissez-faire in practice. The management pendulum had swung from one extreme to the other in the 1960s and 1970s. The iron fist was replaced with the iron fist wrapped in a velvet glove, because management was still in charge in this closed system approach.

The era of que sera sera and open-concept schools and quality circles had run its course. Again, a new model was developed—the neoclassical approach. This was the Ronald Regan era of the 1980s where accountability and assessment ruled the day, but now the model took advantage of the expertise of the professional educator. Still, it was closed model of mechanistic control, as the pendulum had swung back.

Douglas McGregor developed his seminal study of management with his descriptions of the binary Theory X and Theory Y to understand supervisory approaches to human motivation. Theory X managers follow the more classical physics approach of supervising employees, where Theory Y managers deal more in the relational realm of administration. The basic features of Theory X include:

(1) Average workers are by nature indolent—they work as little as possible.
(2) They lack ambition, dislike responsibility, prefer to be led.
(3) They are inherently self-centered, indifferent to organizational needs.
(4) They are by nature resistant to change.
(5) They are gullible, not very bright, ready dupes of the charlatan and demagogue.

The basic features of Theory Y include:

(1) Management is responsible for organizing the elements of production enterprise—money, materials, equipment, people—in the interest of economic (educational) ends.
(2) People are *not* by nature passive or resistant to organizational needs. If they appear so, it is as a result of experience in organizations.
(3) The motivation, potential for development, the capacity for assuming responsibility, the readiness to direct behaviors toward organizational goals are all present in people; management does not put them there. It is a responsibility of management to make it all possible for people to recognize and develop these human characteristics for themselves.
(4) The essential task of management is to arrange organizational conditions and methods of operation so that people can achieve their own goals *best* by directing *their* own efforts toward organizational objectives (all emphasis in original).[31]

With all that is said, Theory X simply states employees are lazy and need to be supervised. Theory Y, on the other hand, sees employees as hardworking and loyal to their institutions. The former model relies on extrinsic motivation, while the latter expects the administration to support intrinsic approaches.

Should an employee exhibit Theory X characteristics, it is because they have been oppressed by supervisors and a system that does not embrace and support individualism, creativity, and autonomy. Considering higher education relies on a highly educated and professional workforce, Theory Y clearly would best be suited for colleges. Unfortunately, Theory X is used more often than naught.

VESTIGES OF THE CLASSICAL ADMINISTRATIVE MODEL

Few university leaders would consider themselves of the "old school." They feel they take into account the informal organization and treat people with dignity. To varying degrees, they are correct. In other words, most administrators are more eclectic in style and are more likely to practice situational leadership, and to some degree distributive leadership. They use a combination of Classical, Human Relations, and Neoclassical approaches—all Closed Systems models—to lead their institutions.

Still, as a matter of fact, much of their practice is more classical than they might want to admit, even in these times of shared decision-making, peer review, accreditation, and professional association. To give a flavor of these remnants of classical organizational thought, and without belaboring the point, a few examples are worth sharing.

Our leaders work within systems that are highly, and rigidly, structured. The hierarchy is a top-down model wherein different silos (colleges, schools, departments) are aligned for efficiency and standardization. All colleges and universities have a president at the top of the pyramid. Directly under them are area vice presidents who have people in specialized functions reporting to them. Within this grand pyramid, are smaller pyramids, with each division leader having a span of control of five to ten people. If too many individuals reside within a department, subunits will propagate. To wit, the organizational blueprint remains cast in stone.

Standardization, routinization, accountability, and policy rule the day. Universities all share common configurations of academic affairs, business affairs, student affairs, enrollment management, and advancement and development. Each division will follow "best practice" (better defined as "common practice"), external and internal rules, laws, and regulations, and policy manuals and procedures. In the contemporary setting of higher education, a person could easily flow from one organization into another with a shallow learning curve.

DRAWBACKS OF THE CLASSICAL ADMINISTRATIVE MODEL

As has been stipulated earlier, the classical bureaucratic model for our organizations is deeply flawed. One need not look far for examples. Our government's dismal handling of the COVID-19 response, bungling of emergency relief efforts after Hurricane Katrina and the hurricane and subsequent earthquakes in Puerto Rico are well-known examples. Margaret Wheatley explained, "[W]e don't have the organizational structures or the leadership that can respond quickly and well to these emergencies. . . . Following any disaster, we see the best of human nature and the worst of bureaucracy."[32]

Indeed, such a lack of responsiveness and an impersonal ethos has turned the public and employees against their very own institutions. "In our Western culture, which is still dominated by the mechanistic, fragmented view of the world, an increasing number of people have seen this as the underlying reason for the widespread dissatisfaction in our society," according to Capra.[33] Peter Block went even further: "Autocratic governance withers the spirit . . . centralized control cannot create a product, guarantee quality, or serve customers."[34]

Francis Fukuyama outlined scores of historical catastrophes in the realm of politics and economics where centralized control models resulted in disaster. While such control models may be efficient in the short-term, their consequences are devastating. He concluded, "These examples from the communist world suggested at one time that the progressive unfolding of modern natural science could just as well lead us to Max Weber's nightmare of a rational and bureaucratized tyranny, rather than to an open, creative and liberal society."[35]

More simply, bureaucracies are too unwieldy and cannot take advantage of the professional expertise and development of their employees. St. John explained this notion: "The goal of enabling professional growth through adapting organizational strategy to meet new challenges may be the optimal vehicle for change in professional organizations. However, this potential is difficult to realize if central strategic decisions and professional actions are tightly regulated and controlled."[36]

All this hard work to create organizations which can be more efficient, effective, and predictable struggles in its pragmatism. Again, we turn to Fukuyama: "Past a certain point, large bureaucracies become increasingly less efficient . . . and are therefore less efficient than a larger number of smaller organizations."[37] Peter Block extended this notion: "We have intentionally structured our organizations so as to exclude lower levels . . . those doing the core work, from planning, organizing, and controlling their work. . . . Having one group manage and one group execute is the death knell of the entrepreneurial spirit."[38]

The challenges to make the requisite changes are manifold. Our training, our experiences—our mimetic isomorphisms—are all that we know. And, a primary counterforce to implementing a new model is the fact that, quite frankly, it's difficult to change the rules of organizations, because the people who played by the rules to get to the top won't want us to change the rules once they get there.

K. C. Cole gives us a cautionary note:

> "*Newton's view [has] prevailed. Indeed, most people today still believe in their heart of hearts that absolute space and time are somehow 'out there,' fixed and immortal, serving as guide stars that keep us from going astray as we grope through the universe. These people are going to have to hang onto their hats.*"[39]

ESSAY—JAIME HUNT

Most people are uncomfortable with change. This prickly reality can create significant challenges in leading an organization. When people are determined to do things "the way they have always been done," unsurprisingly, the organization stagnates. Innovation cannot thrive amid routine. Processes, policies, and practices must not only be flexible, they must also be continually evaluated. The challenge comes when people become attached to processes and policies and cannot rise above the trees to see the forest.

Those who are gifted—or cursed, depending on your perspective—with an innate desire to shake things up can often find themselves frustrated as they watch colleagues fall into stasis. They become irritated when they ask why something is done a particular way and hear a defensive, "We've always done it this way" in response. They approach cyclical projects and tasks—and everything about higher education is cyclical—with a desire to improve upon the previous cycle and break new ground. Again and again they bring new ideas to the table, even if they are frequently shot down.

If this sounds familiar to you, congratulations. You're a change agent.

If it doesn't, that's okay. You can become one.

There are some critical traits that change agents must possess:

1. You must appreciate these five words: More voices at the table.
2. You must be willing to rethink *everything*.

Higher education is often structured to defeat change due to two very specific features endemic to the industry: silos and rigid hierarchy. A colleague of mine once described a college campus as, "A group of independent franchisees all doing their own thing." This feels very much like reality. Even the way most universities describe their structures supports silos. The DIVISION of Academic Affairs. The DIVISION of Advancement. It often truly seems like we are divided. Rather than being a team of teams, we are all pulling in our own directions with our own objectives and our own strategies. These structural divides make interdisciplinary collaboration difficult and they make it very hard to evaluate our practices to identify areas that would benefit from improvement. They also hinder innovation, limit access to alternative perspectives and invite territoriality.

Some might argue that the principle of shared governance "proves" that we are a collaborative group of colleagues. After all, we discuss things (sometimes ad nauseum), we have infinite committees, and we have rooms with walls of whiteboards to capture our brainstormed pearls of wisdom. Unfortunately, even within our own units and divisions silos and hierarchy remain. I urge leaders to look at their own teams. Do assignments cross areas within the unit? Does the teamwork together to make projects more successful? Or is the org chart a series of silos? Are only those at the top of the org chart invited to have a voice at the table? And when we give people a voice, are we only doing it to check a box?

Creativity, ingenuity, and innovation do not only come from the top. Those who rest at the top of the organization chart ascended to these positions in myriad ways. Being a vice anything doesn't automatically mean an individual is forward-thinking or a change agent. You will find trailblazers throughout the organization, but you have to be willing to look, you have to be willing to listen, and you have to be willing to collaborate. Silos must die.

Let me give you a hypothetical example of the way silos fail students. At the start of each semester, Student Accounts offices all over the country send students their tuition bills. At many campuses, a majority of students are reliant on financial aid to pay their bills; however, these two departments fall into different silos on the org chart. Maybe the student received her financial aid information two weeks before her bill arrived, or maybe she got it two weeks later. Or the bill came in the mail but the financial aid information came via email. Now the student is digging through a pile of papers or searching through her email to find what she needs to take the next step in enrollment.

To a lot of people, it makes perfect sense that financial aid and student accounts would send separate communications. They are different offices, many times under different vice presidents. Of course they send different messages. But that line of thinking doesn't serve our students. When a student and his family get a bill they want to know immediately what their options are for paying that bill. They want to know how to apply for aid and the process for accomplishing that. They don't want to wade through our website or dig through their inbox. They want to know right now.

Billing season is a perfect time for cross-campus collaboration. The tuition bill might be the most important document we send our students and their families. How can the offices responsible for sending bills partner with the offices that help families pay them? How can we bring front-line staff—the ones who actually interact with students and speak with families—into the discussion?

Those of us with positions at the lofty top of the organization chart often spend the majority of our days in meetings with other executives. Many leaders often openly acknowledge that they feel meetings with people who are "beneath them" to be, well, beneath them. They couldn't be further from the truth.

Jane, the accounting assistant, spends hours on the phone during billing season helping parents decipher their tuition bill. Doug, the assistant director of financial aid, is on the phone with the Department of Education three times a week, seeking answers to student questions. Brenda, a receptionist in student affairs, chats with students as they wait for their meeting with the dean of students. All of these individuals have powerful insights into the student experience; however, none of the three has a voice at the leadership table. Our organizations are worse for it.

We have to rethink how we approach our work and our relationships. At a previous institution, the executive who led the organization into which I fell told me once that I shouldn't have lunch with someone who falls below me on the organization chart. Another leader once declared she was offended that I copied a "subordinate" on an email to her. These are ridiculous assertions. Meaningful collaboration requires relationships. It requires that we are yoked side-by-side with people we trust and—dare I say—like. These relationships cannot be transactional. They must be authentic and rely on mutual respect. That means getting to know your colleagues and putting in the work to understand their drivers.

When you are able to achieve real collaboration, it feels like magic. Ideas flow as people feel heard. Solutions appear for problems that seemed insurmountable. It just feels *good*. And, it's contagious.

A few years ago, I pulled together a working group of frontline people to rethink how we communicated enrollment steps to incoming first-year students. During our first meeting, the tension in the room was palpable. There were some strained relationships and people were clearly expecting me to dictate the end result of the project. As we move through the process over a period of two months, the emotional weight in the room grew lighter and lighter. People came out of their shells as they saw that not only was their input requested, it was valued. Ideas flowed and solutions were formed. It felt like magic.

In a way, it is magic. I think of the phrase: The whole is greater than the sum of its parts. For that to be true, we have to value not only the individual components, but also the incredible beauty in the way they work together. Throwing vice presidents, directors, executive assistants, instructors, and deans together may seem like an opportunity for chaos. Perhaps it is chaos—but it's the kind of chaos that leads to positive transformation.

LESLIE'S LAMENT

Leslie's daughter's volleyball team wasn't too competitive this year, but the girls were close friends with each other. Leslie sat alone, yet she was surrounded by fellow parents. The parents put on a positive vibe for their daughters—cheering all good effort. Suddenly the whistle let out a shrill warning.

The gym fell quiet, followed by gasps. Then, loud crying from the floor. Girls from both teams quickly gathered together around one girl who was writhing on the floor in pain. Coaches from both teams joined. Michelle, Chrissey's best friend, had injured her knee. They didn't know it now, but they would learn later this evening, Michelle had torn her ACL. As girls from both teams carried Michelle off the court, all with tears in their eyes, parents stood and clapped.

As the game resumed, numerous thoughts flooded Leslie's mind. She was horrified for Michelle and hoped she could recover. Leslie reflected and thought things were so much different with today's generation. "You would never see such empathy from the opponents when I played," Leslie thought to herself. She was proud of these girls.

While the girls showered in the locker room after the game, Leslie remained alone with her thoughts. Chrissey would be taking her SATs this weekend and beginning her search for colleges. Where would she go? The day's board meetings filtered back into her mind. So much to take in.

"All I really want is for Chrissey to be happy," Leslie murmured.

"That's all that any of us want for our kids," laughed LaShonda.

Leslie didn't know she was thinking out loud. LaShonda was Leslie's oldest friend. They both were both activity in the community.

LaShonda added, "I also want Tonyae to be safe when she goes to college and study what she wants to major in."

"I hear you, Shon," Leslie replied. "I agree with that, and I want her to be prepared to find a good job so she can take care of herself." Leslie also thought to herself, but was embarrassed to add, "I want her to be a good citizen, a good person."

Then, LaShonda concluded: "How about we get together for lunch on Monday and catch up?" Leslie agreed and the friends walked out of the gym with their daughters.

Chrissey and Leslie enjoyed the traditional post-match dinner at Luigi's Pizzaria. They talked about the match, spent a good amount of time talking about Michelle's injury, and about the homework that Chrissey had yet to complete tonight. But, they spent the last few minutes talking about college.

"Mom, do we have to talk about college, now?"

"No, but I'm just curious what you're looking for in college," came Leslie's persistent reply.

"I want a lot. I want to get involved in things on campus; I want to play volleyball; and, I want to use my time to do something important with my life. I mean, our environment is the biggest thing for me. I want to make a difference. That's why I want to major in eco-business."

"This generation certainly is more altruistic and service-oriented than my generation," Leslie thought to herself. But, she smiled and replied, "I love you, Chrissey. I'm so proud of you. Let's make this happen."

As they walked to their car, Leslie's mind jumped to her new role on the board of trustees. "How can I help all the students meet their dreams and ambitions?"

NOTES

1. Albert Einstein, *The Theory of Relativity and other Essays* (New York: MJF Publishing, 1950), 22, 28.

2. Perry Rettig, *Quantum Leaps in School Leadership* (Lanham, MD: Rowman & Littlefield, 2002), 3. Much of the early portion of chapter 1 is derived from this original book.

3. Leonard Shlain, *The Alphabet Versus the Goddess: The Conflict between Word and Image* (New York: Penguin Putnam, 1998), 378.

4. Henry Stapp, *Mind, Matter, and Quantum Mechanics* (New York: Springer-Verlag, 1993), 13.

5. Stephen Covey, *The Seven Habits of Highly Effective People* (New York: Fireside of Simon & Schuster, 1990), 169.

6. Margaret Wheatley, *Leadership and the New Science: Learning about Organizations from an Orderly Universe* (San Francisco: Berrett-Koehler, 2000), 6.

7. Peter Senge, *The Fifth Discipline: The Art and Practice of the Learning Organization* (New York: Doubleday/Currency, 1990), 3.

8. Bruce Lipton, *The Biology of Belief: Unleashing the Power of Consciousness, Matter & Miracles* (New York: Hay House, 2008),10.

9. Fritjof Capra and Pier Luigi Luisi, *The Systems View of Life: A Unifying Vision* (Cambridge, United Kingdom: Cambridge University Press, 2014), 14.

This has resulted in differential power structure between the men and women, according to these authors.

10. Capra and Luisi, *Systems View of Life*, 47.

Capra and Luisi conclude, however: "Like most Cartesian economic thought, it [Keynesian economics] has outlived its usefulness."

11. Lipton, *The Biology of Belief*, 72.

12. Edward St. John, *College Organization and Professional Development: Integrating Moral Reasoning and Reflective Practice* (New York: Routledge, 2009), 119.

13. Yuval Levin, *A Time to Build: From Family and Community to Congress and the Campus, How Recommitting to our Institutions can Revive the American Dream* (New York: Basic Books, 2020).

14. J. A. Bransford, A. Brown, and A. Cocking (Eds). *How People Learn: Brain, Mind, Experience, and School* (Washington, DC: National Academy Press, 1999), 6.

15. Robert Owens, *Organizational Behavior in Education: Adaptive Leadership and School Reform* (New York: Pearson Allyn & Bacon, 2004), 83.

16. Reginald Green, *Practicing the Art of Leadership: A Problem-Based Approach to Implementing the ISLLC Standards* (Upper Saddle River, NJ: Merrill Prentice Hall, 2001), 53.

17. Peter Blau, *The Organization of Academic Work* (New York: Wiley, 1973).

18. Peter Block, *Stewardship: Choosing Service over Self-Interest* (San Francisco: Berrett-Koehler, 1996), 101.

Block went further, "The governance system we have inherited and continue to create is based on sovereignty and a form of intimate colonialism . . . We govern our organizations by valuing above all else, consistency, control, and predictability" (7).

19. St. John, *College Organization and Professional Development*.

20. James March and Johan Olsen, *Democratic Governance* (New York: The Free Press, 1995), 79.

21. Charles Heckscher, "Defining the Post-Bureaucratic Type," in *The Post-Bureaucratic Organization: New Perspectives on Organizational Change*, ed. Charles Heckscher and Anne Donnellon (Thousand Oaks, CA: Sage, 1994), 37.

22. Carol Gilligan, *In a Different Voice: Psychological Theory and Women's Development* (Harvard University Press, 2003).

Capra and Luisi added:

Power, in the sense of domination over others, is excessive self-assertion. The social structure in which it is exerted most effectively is the hierarchy. Indeed, our political, military, and corporate structures are hierarchically ordered, with men generally occupying the upper levels and women the lower.

Capra and Luisi, *Systems View of Life*, 14.

23. Mihalyi Csikszentmihalyi, *Flow: The Psychology of Optimal Experience* (New York: Harper Collins, 1990), 78.

24. Francis Neumann, Jr., "Organizational Structures to Match the New Information-Rich Environments: Lessons from the Study of Chaos," *Public Productivity and Management Review*, 21 (September 1997), 90.

25. Tom Nichols, *The Death of Expertise: The Campaign Against Established Knowledge and Why it Matters* (New York: Oxford University Press, 2017).

This weariness of the public to core institutions is also exposed by:

Levin, *A Time to Build*.

26. St. John, *College Organization and Professional Development*, 119.

27. Francis Fukuyama, *The End of History and the Last Man* (New York: The Free Press, 1992), 90.

28. Wayne Hoy and Cecil Miskel, *Educational Administration: Theory, Research, and Practice* (New York: Random House, 1982), 8–9.

29. Jean Lipman-Blumen, *The Connective Edge: Leading in an Interdependent World* (San Francisco: Jossey-Bass, 1996), 62.

30. Lipman-Blumen, *The Connective Edge*, 62.

31. Thomas Sergiovanni and Robert Starratt, *Supervision: A Redefinition* (New York: McGraw-Hill, 1993), 15–16.

32. Wheatley, *Leadership and the New Science*, 171.

Wheatley went further:

Yet these self-organized efforts [of local citizens] are often hindered by officials who refuse their offers, cite regulations, or insist that protocols and procedures be followed (173). . . . In the days after Hurricane Katrina, the blindness was coupled with bureaucratic conditioning and cumbersome chains of command. Missteps, misperceptions, and inaction cascaded through organizations, creating only more chaos (174) . . . Senior leaders find it difficult to act this spontaneous [as local units can] or independently. Any independent response is constrained by the need to maintain power and policies of the organization (175).

33. Fritjof Capra, *The Tao of Physics: An Exploration of the Parallels between Modern Physics and Eastern Mysticism* (Boston: Shambhala, 2000), 25.

Capra expressed his concern even with his physicist colleagues: "All these developments strongly indicated that the simple mechanistic picture of basic building blocks had to be abandoned, and yet many physicists are still reluctant to do so" (285).

34. Block, *Stewardship*, 8.
35. Fukuyama, *The End of History*, 90.
36. St. John, *College Organization and Professional Development*, 119.

He explained, "It is a challenge for strategic organizations to create the openness necessary to enable communities of practice to respond to initiatives and create new pathways to success" (167).

37. Fukuyama, *The End of History*, 78.

To which he added, "Centralized economies have not succeeded in making rational investment decisions. . . . The complexity of modern economies proved to be simply beyond the capabilities of centralized bureaucracies to manage" (93).

38. Block, *Stewardship*, 45, 46.

Block specified: "Two problems with having a managerial class are that it is too expensive and it creates obstacles to improving quality, to give customers what they want, and to succeeding in a volatile and unpredictable marketplace" (46); and, "The governance system we grew up with cannot deliver quality, costs too much, and is ill-suited to meet the need for rapid change" (49).

39. K. C. Cole, *The Hole in the Universe: How Scientists Peered over the Edge of Emptiness and Found Everything* (New York: Harcourt, 2001), 37.

Margaret Wheatley went further:

The real world stands in stark and absolute contrast to the world invented by Western thought. We believe that people, organizations, and the world are machines, and we organize massive systems to run like clockwork in a steady-state world. The leader's job is to create stability and control, because without human intervention, there is no hope for order. Without strong leadership everything falls apart. It is assumed that most people are dull, not creative, that people need to be bossed around, that new skills develop only through training. People are motivated using fear and rewards; internal motivators such as compassion and generosity are discounted. These beliefs have created a world filled with disengaged workers who behave like robots, struggling in organizations that become more chaotic and ungovernable over time.

Wheatley, *Leadership and the New Science*, 170–171.

Chapter 2

You've Got a New Thing Coming

"*Matter itself does not behave like a machine at all. The very mechanical premises upon which science has been built may be overturned by science itself.*"[1]

What an astonishing proclamation by Jeffrey Santinover, author of *The Quantum Brain*, to introduce this chapter. New science is overthrowing our foundational understandings of the old sciences. With that said, a new understanding of our organizations and leadership must jettison old foundational principles and look for new models.

According to Roland Omnes, "There is no doubt that we are going through a period of fracture. . . . A strange predominance of abstractness, of formalness, exists as the very heart of reality. There can be only one remedy: to invent a new way of understanding."[2] This is precisely the aim of chapter 2—to begin with a new understanding of science, and then to reimagine a new way of structuring and leading our institutions of higher learning, via a Thought Experiment, if you will. The eminent new leadership visionary, Margaret Wheatley extolled:

> People often comment that the new leadership I propose couldn't possibly work in the "real world." I assume they are referring to their organization or government, a mechanistic world managed by bureaucracy, governed by policies and laws, filled with people who do what they're told, who surrender their freedom to leaders and sit passively waiting for instructions. . . . This is not the real world. This world is a manmade, dangerous fiction that destroys our capacity to deal well with what's really going on. The real world, not this fake one, demands that we learn to cope with chaos, that we understand what motivates humans.[3]

In *The Tao of Physics*, Fritjof Capra added, "In modern physics, the image of the universe as a machine has been replaced by that of an interconnected, dynamic whole whose parts are essentially interdependent and have to be understood as patterns of a cosmic *process* (emphasis added"[4]). In a concurring opinion, Michael Talbot noted, "Indeed, [quantum physicist David] Bohm believes that our almost universal tendency to fragment the world and ignore the dynamic interconnectedness of all things is responsible for many of our problems, not only in science but in our lives and our society as well."[5]

It is time to now get down to brass tacks. Just what are these new sciences, and what lessons can we learn from them? Einstein's foundational theories of relativity will serve as a primer to launch a discussion of quantum physics. That will then be complemented with a discussion in chapter 3 of the other new sciences and their implications.

ALBERT EINSTEIN AND RELATIVITY

Einstein's special and general theories of relativity were developed from his study of Michael Faraday's conceptualization of electric and magnetic field theory. K. C. Cole explained, "Faraday, in effect, shifted the burden of reality from the particle to the things that emanate from it. The space between the particles became primary."[6]

In Einstein's own words, "The name 'theory of relativity' is connected with the fact that motion from the point of view of possible experience always appears as the *relative* motion of one object with respect to another. . . . Motion is never observable as 'motion with respect to space.'"[7] This led Einstein to add a fourth dimension—that of time. Space and time are relative to the observer and one dimension cannot be considered without the other.

The notion of relativity is best explained by Omnes: "There is neither absolute space nor absolute time; only measures of distance and time depending on the motion of the observer. The way measures taken by two different observers are related only involves the velocity of each one with respect to the other, that is, their *relative* motion."[8] It needs to be made clear that this fourth dimension of time is not just another dimension to consider. It is central to the other three dimensions of space; space cannot be considered, in other words, without time. Time is central in this interwoven spacetime continuum.

Fritjof Capra explained Einstein's subsequent theory of general relativity as an extension of special relativity to include gravity. "The force of gravity, according to Einstein, has the effect of 'curving' space and time. This means that ordinary Euclidean geometry is no longer valid in such a curved space, just as two-dimensional geometry of a plane cannot be applied on the surface of a sphere."[9] He continued, "In general relativity, the gravitational field and the structure . . . of space are identical."[10] As gravity can curve or warp both space and time, it can thus alter our perceptions of space and time. This then led to Einstein's prediction of black holes.

From Einstein's work on relativity, we have learned some life lessons. We know that observation is relative from person-to-person, and across space (e.g., across the entire organization,), and across time (not just a moment in time, but over extended periods), as these concepts are all relative to one another. Also, individuals can observe or have different perceptions of reality. We further know that *process* is a critical and central feature to creation, to creativity. We also now recognize that nothing exists without relationships to something else. Later, we will discuss the profound implications for our institutions.

Before moving onto a discussion of quantum physics, a note from K. C. Cole is appropriate. "Einstein's theory of gravity (general relativity) perfectly describes everything that happens on large scales in the cosmos. Quantum mechanics perfectly describes everything else."[11] Cole further explains that nature creates in space, which is a lesson for our organizations—we need space in order to create (both time and place). Theoretical physicist at Columbia University, Brian Greene, made special note of the science, as well as a hint toward implications for the way we view our work:

> The meta-lesson of both relativity and quantum mechanics is that when we deeply probe the fundamental workings of the universe we may come upon aspects that are vastly different from our expectations. The boldness of asking deep questions may require unforeseen flexibility if we are to accept the answers.[12]

In *The Tao of Physics*, Fritjof Capra extended this line of thinking:

> The discoveries of modern physics necessitated profound changes of concepts like space, time, matter, object, cause and effect, etc., and since these concepts are so basic to our way of experiencing the world it is not surprising that the physicists who were forced to change them felt something of a shock. Out of these changes emerged a new and radically different world view.[13]

QUANTUM PHYSICS

In the quantum world, reality doesn't appear or act like what we have learned over the years. There is this quantum strangeness that scientists talk about. In *The Quantum Brain*, Jeffrey Santinover wrote, "At the cellular level, matter itself actually looks and behaves . . . 'more like a thought' than like cogs of a machine." He then noted, "A number of the founders of quantum mechanics wondered out loud whether the ancient mystics might not be right after all."[14]

The quantum world is a world of probabilities. Santinover explained, "In a quantum regime, even in the theoretical extreme where you know everything there is to know about it, you absolutely cannot predict the outcome—just the probabilities of various outcomes."[15] The science looks at the interconnectedness of the universe; its language is the more intuitive and qualitative mathematics of patterns and relationships.[16] In 1996, Capra explained:

> In the formalism of quantum theory these relationships are expressed in terms of probabilities, and the probabilities are determined by the dynamics of the whole system. Whereas in classical mechanics the properties and behavior of the parts determine those of the whole, the situation is reversed in quantum mechanics: it is the whole that determines the behavior of the parts.[17]

In other words, the parts are so interwoven with all the other parts that their very existence and behavior are governed by the whole system. When viewing a part in isolation, the observer does not see the part as it really exists. The part behaves differently when it is isolated that it does when it is integrated with the whole. Plucking, or observing, one strand of the system shakes the entire web.

The ancient Sufi story of six blind men who happen upon an elephant comes to mind. Each blind man reaches out to touch a different part of the elephant. One man feels the oak-like stature of the leg, while another feels the heavy coarse skin. Still another holds the elephant's strong and flexible trunk, while another holds its ropelike tail. Similarly, another man feels its rigid tusks, and another feels its expansive and thin ears.

Each man has certainly felt the elephant but knows not the elephant. In isolation, each part is different but does not show the true essence of what it is to be an elephant. When all the parts are living and breathing together, we can have a clearer understanding of what it is to be an elephant. In the immortal words of Anaxagoras, "All things will be in everything; nor is it possible for them to be apart, but all things have a portion of everything."

Indeed, the quantum world does not fit our understanding of what we experience at least through the lens of what we have been taught—our mimetic isomorphism. But, maybe this quantum reality actually is a better fit for our intuitive and human existence, and of our human organizations. Our quantum physicist peers have prepared some experiments, both theoretical and real, to help us understand this reality.

DOUBLE-SLIT EXPERIMENT

According to theoretical physicist and cofounder of string field theory Michio Kaku, "One of the essential postulates of the quantum theory is that matter can exhibit both wave-like and particle-like characteristics,"[18] both at the same time. The double-slit experiment proves this postulate. "It's true that all the mystery of quantum mechanics is contained in the double-slit experiment," according to Jeffrey Santinover, author of the *Quantum Brain*.[19]

Imagine a light beam pointed directly at a vertical surface (figure 2.1). The surface has two slits that can allow the light beam to pass through it, either through one slit at a time or through both slits simultaneously. There is a recording device behind the surface; this device measures whether the light behaves like individual particles or is diffuse representing wave-like characteristics. If only one slit is open, the light will land on the recording device and be measured as individual particles. If, on the other hand, both slits are open, the light will land on the recording device and be measured as a wave.

What makes this experiment so confounding is the fact that the light beam behaves in such a way as to suggest it knows whether one or both slits are open, and even more confounding, that it is being observed. The light coming is both a wave and particles, at the same time. This concept, theorized by Niels Bohr, is known as the Principle of Complementarity,[20] wherein light contains dualistic attributes—particles and waves. But, because of the experiment and observation, it collapses into one or the other state. If not observed, it would continue being both wave- and particle-like. The act of observation delimits the probability function. At that moment, only one reality will then exist.

Taking this duality a step further, Capra stipulated, "As in quantum theory, the field . . . is not only the underlying essence of all material objects, but also carries their mutual interactions in the form of waves. The field is a continuum which is present everywhere in space and yet in its particle aspects has a discontinuous, 'granular' structure. These two apparently contradictory concepts are thus unified and seen to be merely different aspects of the same reality."[21] To which he summarized, "Opposites . . . are merely two sides of the same reality, extreme parts of a single whole."[22] In practical terms, Omnes noted:

> Complementarity was at the basis of Bohr's argument against naïve versions of realism. . . . [O]ne may consider some properties of a logical system and deal with them in a logically consistent way, but that often there are completely different consistent histories incompatible with the first ones.[23]

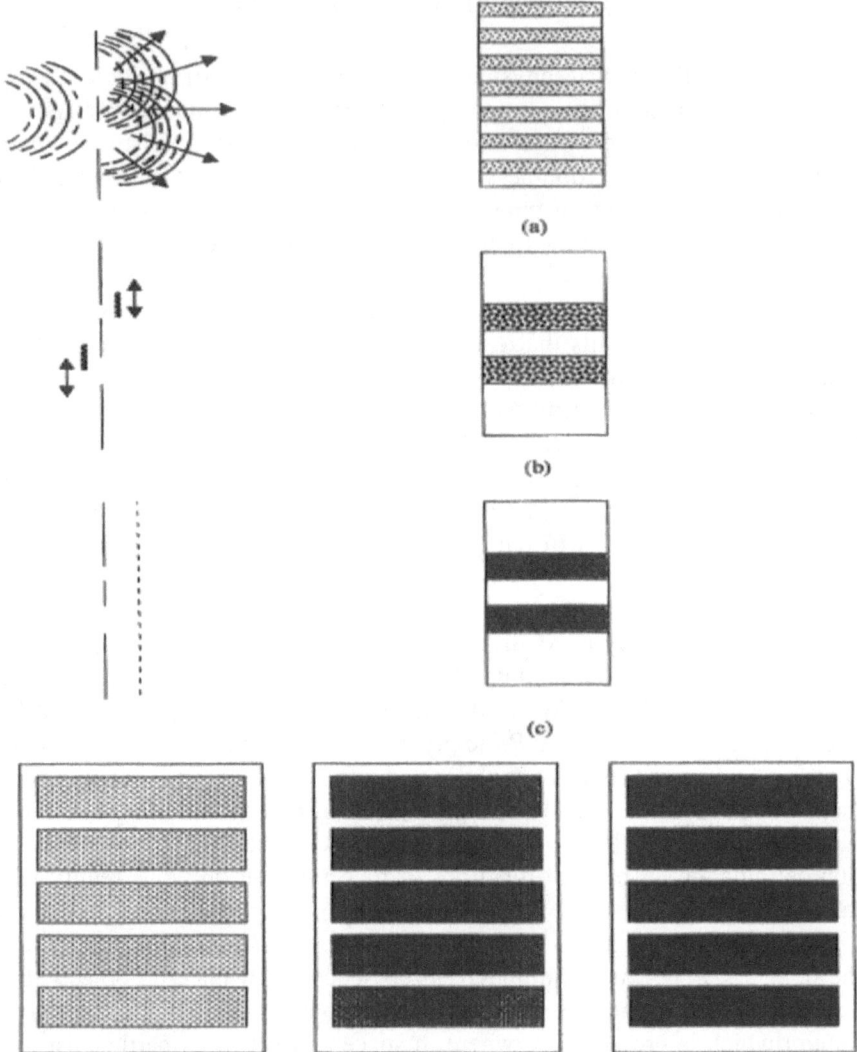

Figure 2.1 Double-Slit Experiment. *Source*: Ronald Pine. *Science and the Human Prospect* Belmont, CA: Wadsworth, 2000), 245. Copyright 2000 by Ronald C. Pine. Reprinted with permission.

But there is another critical lesson to be learnt from this experiment—that of the impact of the observer in the system. "The universal interwovenness revealed by quantum theory always includes the human observer and his or her consciousness."[24] The fact is inescapable—the observer impacts the experiment. In our organizations, each participant has an impact whether or not it can be seen. The very nature of the intentions of our observations, what and how we assess, will impact the task at hand.

Our Newtonian way of thinking has led us to believe that atoms can only be particles or only wave-like at any given moment. In reality, they are both particles and waves concurrently. Niels Bohr found no problem with this duality in nature. He coined the term, "complementarity" to explain the notion that nature needs both sides of this coin. They are different but not separate. Both need one another—they complement each other. However, our observations limit our views and perceptions to seeing only one of the concurrent aspects at a time.

With this complementarity came an associated concept known as the Heisenberg Uncertainty Principle. It shows us a conundrum of our classical approach to studying nature. Since we know that anything has multiple characteristics, and since we know that we can only study one aspect at a time, we will never be able to understand or observe the entire system as a unified whole.[25] Heisenberg theorized that we can only observe the location of an atom or the speed of the atom at a given moment. We cannot observe both at the same time. So, we can know its location, but not its speed, or vice versa. Our observation/understanding is limited.

"Heisenberg's remarkable discovery was," according to Gary Zukav, "that there are limits beyond which we cannot measure accurately. . . . There exists an ambiguity barrier beyond which we never can pass without venturing into the realm of uncertainty . . . the 'uncertainty principle.'"[26] Yet, we continue to build our organizations and our strategic plans with certainty, control, and data analytics. While these may be important, they are insufficient, and our measurements miss as much, if not more, than they capture.

SCHRODINGER'S CAT

The now famous Schrodinger's Cat has also created quite a dilemma for quantum physicists. Austrian physicist Erwin Schrodinger designed an imaginary or theoretical experiment wherein a live cat was placed inside a box. A mechanism triggers the release of either food or deadly cyanide pellets. Now the conundrum. Through mathematical figuring—known as a "probability function"—Schrodinger showed that after the trigger has released its food or poison the cat is both alive and dead at the same time that is until the observer opens the box. At the instant of observation, the cat is then observed as either alive or dead and the alternate chance is gone forever.

Schrodinger's Cat has now become a reality. While there is no real cat, the theoretical construct has now been proven in physics laboratories. Gary

Taubes reported that physicists at the National Institute of Standards and Technology in Boulder, Colorado have been able to:

> trap a single beryllium ion in an electromagnetic cage, excite it into a superposition of internal electronic quantum states, then ease those two states apart so that the atom appears to be in two distinct physical locations simultaneously. The result can be considered the anti-vivisectionist version of the dead-and-alive superposition of cat states.[27]

Atoms can be described as packets of potentialities and can occupy several different orbits at one time. This complementarity principle has been coupled together with Schrodinger's Cat. Philip Yam reported similar work by David Pritchard and other physicists at the Massachusetts Institute of Technology. With the use of lasers, these scientists have been able to cool atoms and move them around. In Yam's words:

> Physicists have . . . created small-scale Schrodinger's cats. These "cats" were individual electrons and atoms made to reside in two places simultaneously, and electromagnetic fields excited to vibrate in two different ways at once.[28]

These findings reinforce the notions of probabilities and potentialities. Everything exists simultaneously as a packet of potentials. Quantum physicists call this "the state vector." This is the point in which something is suspended in all its potential phases. However, at the point of observation, we get "state vector collapse." Or the point in which all the possible outcomes collapse into one state—the state that we see.

Again, there is more than one way to view and understand nature (and our systems), and each thing or action does not exist as only one reality until the act of observation. In other words, the observer and the act of observation help to create reality. By our very act of observation, we help to create reality. We lose something when we make an observation or measurement; we miss more than we see. What's more, we might not even be able to make wholly accurate judgments about the differences of what we measure.

BELL'S THEOREM

In another experiment, nonlocal causality—or Bell's Theorem, we learn that relationships and interconnectedness are the foundation of all systems. In this theoretical experiment, designed by physicist John Bell and later demonstrated in the laboratory by Thomas Young, two electrons are paired together and given the identical spin on their axes. When they are separated over a great distance in space and then measured, they still have the same spin.

However, if after they are separated, one is given a new spin, the other one will simultaneously change its spin accordingly, on its own. This would suggest that they are communicating over space and time, a time that is faster than the speed of light. Zukav wrote, "In 1972 John Clauser and Stuart Freedman of the Lawrence Berkeley Laboratory actually performed this experiment to confirm or disprove these predictions. They found that the statistical predictions upon which Bell based his theorem *are* correct."[29]

This laboratory experiment has been subsequently replicated on computer chips[30] and explains corresponding processes in the brain with instantaneous feedback loops.[31] This is the notion of inseparability or nonseparability.[32] This quantum entanglement will eventually lead to quantum computers whereby fiber optics will no longer be needed to connect technology at a distance.[33]

Talbot explained, "The apparent separateness of consciousness and matter is an illusion, an artifact that occurs only after both have unfolded into the explicate world of objects and sequential time."[34] In a most perplexing manner, Talbot noted:

> Most of us tend to think of an electron as a tiny sphere or a BB whizzing around, but nothing could be further from the truth . . . physicists have found that *it literally possesses no dimension*. . . . [an electron can manifest as either a particle or a wave]. . . as if it were a wave spread out over space. . . . as a wave can do things no particle can.[35]

Fritjof Capra explained, "Bell's Theorem demonstrates that the universe is fundamentally interconnected, interdependent, and inseparable."[36] Eminent professor of psychology, Mihaly Csikszentmihalyi extended this concept to human endeavors, ". . . from the knowledge scientists and other thinkers . . . we learn that the consequences of actions may not be immediately visible, but may have effects in distant connections, because everything that exists is part of an interconnected system."[37]

In *Synchronicity: The Inner Path of Leadership*, Joseph Jaworski wrote, "The effect is a simple consequence of the oneness of apparently separate objects. It is a quantum loophole through which physics admits the necessity of a unitary vision."[38] Furthermore, *relationship* is the key determiner of what is observed and of how particles manifest themselves. Particles come into being and are observed only in relationship to something else. "They do not exist as independent 'things.'"[39]

One of the most profound implications for human organizations is that space is alive, and this "void" is where creativity occurs. Michael Talbot remarked, "So struck was Bohm by these organic qualities [of electron and ion plasms] that he later remarked he'd frequently had the impression the electron sea was 'alive.'"[40] This led Talbot to note, "Matter does not exist independently from the [metaphorical] sea, from so-called empty space. . . . Space is not empty. It is *full,* a plenum as opposed to a vacuum."[41]

Malin extended this notion to the dynamic, living world. "Process philosophy is a rigorous and inspiring metaphysical system that claims that the universe and its constituents are alive. . . . We live not in a universe of objects but in a universe of experiences."[42] Capra concluded, "the vacuum is truly a 'living Void,' pulsating in endless rhythms of creation and destruction . . . the void has emerged as a dynamic quantity of utmost importance."[43] This whole notion of nothingness leading to creativity, silence leading to thinking—for example, is the central tenet of K. C. Cole's book, *The Whole in the Universe.*[44]

WHY A QUANTUM APPROACH IS NECESSARY FOR UNDERSTANDING PEOPLE

To reiterate, classical physics is an inappropriate approach for the framing of educational leadership models. "Traditional management theory is based on a view of how schools operate that does not fit the real world very well."[45] After a meeting with Japanese businessmen, Joseph Jaworski reflected:

> I was struck, however, from the very outset at how rational the Westerners in the group seemed to be, and how skeptical and even disdainful most of them were of anything that smacked of what they referred to as "the soft stuff"—anything that could not be measured or quantified. Graphs and charts were the order of the day because quantification and measurement were what was seen as real. . . . I had come to see the immeasurable as precisely that which was most real, that which I cared most deeply about. I recalled what Bohm had said about this, "The attempt to suppose that measure exists prior to man and independently of him leads, as has been seen, to the "objectivication" of man's insight so that it becomes rigidified and unable to change, eventually bringing about fragmentation and general confusion."[46]

It seems that the scientific method and the objectification of things have made our institutions so very sterile. Our employees have known this for decades, and social scientists have been calling for changes. Leadership expert, Diane Fassel, wrote about the confusion of our organizations, "Perhaps some of the disequilibrium we are feeling in organizations is that the old organizational diagram is hardwired in our brains, while the actual process we experience is one of relationships."[47]

Intuition is central to quantum organizations. Higher education, though, has been late to realize that intuition is important to leadership. Some of the most highly successful private-sector leaders have understood and embraced this. Leadership theorist Peter Senge posited:

> Intuition in management has recently received increasing attention and acceptance, after many decades of being officially ignored. Now numerous studies show that experienced managers and leaders rely heavily on intuition—that the do not figure out complex problems rationally. They rely on hunches, recognize patterns, and draw intuitive analogies and parallels to other seemingly disparate situations. . . . Their intuition tells them that cause and effect are not close in time and space, that obvious solutions produce more harm than good, and that short-term fixes produce long-term problems.[48]

From Confucius to Radhakrishnan to Toju and others, many ancient Eastern philosophers had cherished intuition, as well. In fact, Sarvepalli Radhakrishnan believed that "intuition enables us to know Reality directly."[49]

Likewise, the feeling of the interconnectedness of the universe "is central to every major religion, including Judaism, Islam, Christianity, Hinduism, Buddhism, and Taoism."[50] According to Pine, "Eastern mysticism is also consistent with the results of quantum physics. The mystics have always rejected the idea of a hidden clockwork mechanism, sitting out there, and independent of human observation."[51] This interconnectedness is crucial to the survival of our organizations and systems. As Capra put forth, "In nature there is no 'above' or 'below,' and there are no hierarchies. There are only networks nesting within other networks."[52]

The interconnectedness in nature and in organizations then tells of the importance of relationships. Margaret Wheatley connected quantum physics to management by stating, "Leadership is now being examined for its relational aspects. . . . If the physics of our universe is revealing the primacy of relationships, is it any wonder that we are beginning to reconfigure our ideas about management in relational terms?"[53] Systems thinkers from Csikszentmihalyi to Covey and from Senge to Block have seen the vital importance of relationships. In the words of Patrick Dolan:

> The first issue of systems-thinking is that the critical phenomena are *not* the individual parts, but how they fit together. This is a network of relationships deeply interconnected. Each one of these "subsystems" is somehow defined by the position of the others.[54]

It would appear quantum physics does seem to be a better match for creating a model of leadership, for working with humans, as opposed to automatons, and their organizations. Quantum physics speaks of relations, interconnectedness, creativity, and the intuition of people.

LESSONS LEARNED

There are so many lessons we should take away from quantum physics. We will find, ultimately, that we have been structuring and leading our organizations in an ineffective manner, but we can make adjustments that will be much more natural and efficacious.

- The whole system is interconnected
- Process is a central feature of creation
- The Fourth Dimension of reality includes Time
- Space and Time are relative and not linear
- The observer is central, and our understanding/perception is relative
- The future is not deterministic, but is a series of potentials/probabilities
- There is a duality in nature with a corresponding complementarity; both dual aspects need one another and are interdependent, yet there is an uncertainty of the whole
- Nonlocal causality is a connection at a distance across the system—an inseparability
- Relationships, interconnectedness is a central feature of systems
- Intuition is equally or more important than observation

In the meantime, we will spend a few minutes reviewing an essay by Rinardo Reddick who spent his entire career in higher education and private-sector management and leadership. We will then continue following the evolving story of Leslie.

> "We are in transition, between an era that has died and one waiting to be born. The hereditary aristocracies have vanished; the new cognitive elite has just begun its ascent to dominance."[55] Jeffrey Santinover

ESSAY—RINARDO REDDICK

The Hook

It feels like yesterday when Roger was completing his master's degree and navigating the job market. He was invited to his very first professional on-campus interview. Roger's stomach was tied in knots, but the blood was flowing with excitement and curiosity. He had two other on-campus interviews and was looking forward to each one.

The first campus visit went very well. He looked for red flags and noticed that there was little diversity at the university. Was it a big deal that he would be the only professional black person on the orientation staff? Roger was offered the job before he left the on-campus interview. After talking to his mentors, Roger accepted the new job!

Shortly after accepting the position, Roger received a phone call from John, who was the assistant director for Student Orientation. John said that he really enjoyed meeting Roger during his interview and felt that Roger would work well "under" him in the Student Orientation Office. John stated that he "liked your energy and what you could bring to the office."

Roger learned that John was an alumnus of the school and worked for the department as a student, until he graduated with his BA degree. All of his experiences were in the same department and same area. Furthermore, John had the same supervisor for most of his professional career. Roger was surprised to hear John say that he did not have a master's degree and that his undergraduate degree was good enough. Roger started his new job in June.

The Wake-Up Call

The professional staff training went well, and John took the time to show Roger what he could before Roger's staff arrived. Furthermore, Roger was excited to hear that he would be working with a graduate assistant. Her name was Julie. Julie was starting later than the others, so Roger wasn't sure what to expect.

While in his office working on a training schedule, Roger heard a knock at his office door. He knew it had to be Julie. With excitement, he opened the door, and saw someone his same race! Being that Roger was the only professional staff of color at that point, he was relieved to know that there were two of them and that they would be working very closely together.

In preparation for the staff, Julie and Roger worked together closely. As Julie and Roger met with John, he indicated that he expected consistency and that the staff should be supervised very similarly. Roger didn't have any issues with this but did ask about flexibility. "Sure," said John, "there is lots of flexibility and you have the ability to do many things with your staff." Roger felt good about that.

John continued to say that "also, you need to know that I will give you everything you need to know as I get it." Again, that made sense to Roger and Julie. John admitted that he had a "hard time of letting go of things, but he would in due time." Roger wasn't very sure what he meant but brushed it aside. As the student staff started to arrive, Julie and Roger were instructed by John to do everything in a specific manner. John stated that "you both need to train the staff by my guidelines and can only meet with them at the set times that I have planned." John desperately tried to control information and processes.

Roger looked at John with confusion. Roger expressed to John that he wanted to follow the expectations of the schedule that were received in professional staff training. John explained that the timeline was not what really works, and they should go with what he had planned instead. John continued to say that "I would have told you sooner about these changes but didn't have enough time to let you know."

John left the room for another meeting. When he left the room, Julie and Roger glanced at each other with expressions of surprise and confusion. Roger leaned over to Julie and whispered, "I feel that all the planning that you and I did just went out the window!" In a very soft-spoken voice, Julie said, "I feel that he did more than just make changes; everything was completely different, and it was all his way!"

It became very clear that John's way was the only acceptable way. John was so invested in the only place that he knew. He became so micromanaging that Roger and Julie had to ask for permission to bake brownies for their staff. His response was, "just as long as Julie does it; you can do it, but you can't bake brownies more than once," with a smile on his face. John believed that "you should not spoil your staff too much; they may get lazy and not want to work, your student development theory doesn't tell you that."

Furthermore, John made sure that Roger and Julie understood "what happens here should stay here. If it doesn't stay here, you make yourself look bad and will lose any control that you have. I may not have a master's degree, but at least I know that! See what extra schooling does for you!" Clearly, John viewed his employees through the lens of Theory X. It was his responsibility to motivate them and to make them work.

Roger and Julie looked at John and were startled. Julie asked John what he meant by that. "You know what I mean; no need to go into details. I am the best teacher you'll ever have. I am teaching you how to be a good employee and how things really work in the real world. I am getting my money's worth from you both. I am sure you will thank me later," with a big grin on his face. He picked up his phone and asked them to close the door behind them.

Follow the Leader

How did Roger and Julie end up in this situation? They decided to talk to another one of the professional staff members, in confidence. The other assistant director, Jake, was very honest with them. Jake stated, "It's important for you to know that John has been in this department since he was an undergraduate student. He has worked here as a student leader and in your current positions."

This was a glaring example of John's mimetic isomorphism. "To work with John, you need to be strong-willed and understand that autonomy is not what John believes in. He works better independently, does not like to be challenged, but requires lots of support. Power is his best friend and enables him to make decisions that affect everyone in his area." In other words, John saw his power derived from his position of formal authority.

Furthermore, he went onto say that every person of color that had worked "for" John left within six months to one year. Oh really? Here they are, in their first professional position and this is their experience? Roger and Julie had no ability to make decisions and no ability to challenge the process. According to the other AD, the department has always known about John and how difficult he can be but appreciated his results, so were willing to look past his issues.

In the middle of November, John asked Roger to come into his office. John gave Roger a letter of probation for "something" that he did back in August, without further explanation. Roger looked at him in disbelief and said, "August? You are giving me this letter, now, in November, for something that you feel that I did wrong in August?" "Yes," John said. Roger looked at him and said, "it's not supposed to be like this."

Roger later ran into Julie. She seemed very irritated and upset. He asked what was wrong. Julie explained that John has just put her on probation because of something that she did back in August! Roger looked at Julie and said, "Seems like he got both of us, huh?" They both walked out with a sense of confusion. They each began to ponder, what kind of leadership is this?

Is this what Leadership Looks Like?

In *The Quantum University*, Perry Rettig examines the traditional systems of leadership and the impact these have on our professional experiences. The story that you just read is based on actual events and examines the intersections of power, authority, professional culture and systematic oppression. Roger and Julie were energized and excited to begin their new professional careers. The expectations that each of them had were based on their academic and professional experiences in environments that were supportive, collaborative, and grounded in student development theory. The reality of their experiences with John left them questioning their higher education socialization and training.

John, however, was completely at home. This was the only professional environment that he had ever experienced. He was valued, because of his results; hence the department was willing and able to ignore his behavior and leadership style. John cared little for collaborative efforts, student theory, and the need to build an environment that was supportive and fostered growth. John only recognized his way and failed to recognize the impact on those around him. The department chose to encourage John's leadership style, as it appeared to benefit the department.

John failed to understand that as the leader, he had the unique ability to motivate those around him and to embrace the common experience in a learning environment. He used his power and authority to "get the job done," with little recognition for the need of working together as a team, embracing democratic principles, and valuing those that worked "for" him. Similar to the central theme presented by Rettig, this story demonstrates the how the traditional ideology of "leadership," may be engrained in forms of systematic and institutionalized forms of oppression.

Roger and Julie were challenged to think about the type of leadership they needed to be successful, or as Rettig describes throughout his work, the type of leadership that most of us reading this book have come to recognize is necessary for professional happiness and success. These excited young professionals, who were excited to make a difference, instead, had to figure out how to find their voice in an environment that thrived on silence, oppression, and micromanagement.

As you think about the central theme of this book, consider the following:

1) How does the author explore the need to reexamine leadership in higher education?
2) In what ways can I reflect upon my own experiences and reposition those experiences to align with this new way of conceptualizing leadership?
3) In what ways, can you use your voice to advocate for the necessary changes in how we engage others to be valued in our various leadership systems? How can you lead up?

How you chose to move forward has a ripple effect on reimaging leadership and that impact has the ability to initiate innovation and excellence.

LESLIE'S LAMENT

LaShonda and Leslie sat in a booth at Los Diablos Mexican Grill. This was always their go-to place. Both typically tried to eat healthy, but on such occasions they would have an excuse to splurge. Today was one of those days.

"How old are we, Leslie," LaShonda began, "that we have daughters getting ready for college?"

"I know; it seems like we ourselves just graduated yesterday," Leslie commiserated.

"And, remember our dreams? You wanted to be a literary giant—to write the great American novel, Leslie. And I—I was going to be the first woman CEO of IBM."

Leslie smiled, "True. While those dreams maybe didn't come true, I do think we were pretty successful, don't you?"

"Oh, no doubt," came LaShonda's reply. "You became an English teacher and you're still working on that novel. But, you did get a few editorials published in the newspaper. And, I may not have ended up at IBM, but I did actually start my own business, eventually."

Leslie followed with, "And, both of us have raised wonderful families. We talked about that when we were roommates. And, both of us are actively involved in our communities. You serve on the Chamber of Commerce board of directors, and I serve on the education committee. You volunteer at the food pantry, and I teach adult education at church. Yeah, I think we're both pretty successful."

While pausing to grab another bite of lunch, both thought of the reason they got together—to talk about their daughters' futures. But, Leslie had a nagging issue that kept creeping into the forefront of her mind.

"Shon, you have a board of directors at your company, and you serve on the Chamber board. How do these boards operate? What are their responsibilities?"

LaShonda blew out a gentle breathe of air. "Gee, Leslie, that's an interesting question. I don't know. Each board is so different, but for the most part their purpose is all the same."

Leslie gave her friend a quizzical look and didn't say a word.

So, LaShonda continued. "Each board is unique and has its own personality. I really think the difference-maker is the chair. You know, if they are a person who runs a tight ship and just gets down to business, or if they are one who embraces sharing and team-work. I guess that makes some old-school and others new-school."

Leslie was filtering these comments through the lens of her recent experience. "I think our university board is old-school, she said to herself." Then, she asked for clarification. "Tell me, Shon, what does the new-school look like?"

"Well, I like to think of my own board as new-school. While the chair and I set the agenda, we have different people be responsible for each agenda item—they own it, so to speak. But, it's more than that. We have taught them to engage everyone, both at the committee level and at the full board. People need to participate, but they need to be prepared ahead of time so that they can participate effectively. That means they read materials and documents ahead of time, they ask questions when they don't know the answers, and they do their homework."

"That's interesting. I mean, that wasn't my experience. My experience was that the board listened to the administration present the items—they, the administration, were large and in charge, so to speak. I kind of had the feeling we were there to affirm and approve," Leslie continued.

"The problem with that," responded LaShonda, "is the administration owns it. They are really the only ones responsible. Ultimately, then, what is the purpose of the board? There really are several purposes to a board. They do serve in an advisory capacity, of course, but there's more to it than that. They want to make certain the administration is beholden to the institution's mission; they want to make certain the institution is maintaining its short-term and long-term financial stability; they hire and evaluate the executive; and they each bring a particular expertise to the board."

Leslie nodded her head while LaShonda spoke; then she thought out loud. "You know, I think I wasn't a very good board member at my first meeting. I mean, I read all my materials, but I hadn't really asked any questions in preparation or during the meeting. I was just not actively engaged. And, I think the administration was totally fine with that."

"Don't be too hard on yourself, Leslie. You did read in preparation. Were you paying attention and really listening during the meetings?"

"Of course," Leslie replied.

"Well, that was your first meeting. You were actively engaged—intellectually. That will help you for future meetings," LaShonda encouraged.

Both women finished up their meals—LaShonda with her veggie burrito and Leslie with her softshell tacos. Leslie then smiled, "Hey, I would love to see your board in action. Could I be a fly on the wall at your next meeting?"

This took LaShonda back for a brief moment. "Wow, that's an interesting request. Yes, I think so. Let me think about it and get back to you. Our next meeting is in three weeks. Now, let's talk about the girls. What are you and Chrissey looking for in your college visits during next week's break?"

"Gee, you know how to change subjects, Shon! Honestly, I don't know if we're looking for the same things. Mostly, I want her to be safe and happy. I want her to feel comfortable to explore, to experience as much as she can, and all of that at a good price. That's the kind of stuff I'll be looking for in her college."

LaShonda continued, "What does Chrissey want to see when she visits campuses?"

"Maybe she wants some of the same things, I guess. I mean, she wants to get very involved in co-curricular things and she wants to make new friends. She definitely wants to major in something where she thinks she can make a difference in the world and to contribute to her community after she graduates. It's so different than our generation. I just wanted to take my classes and get my degree."

"I hear you, Leslie," LaShonda replied. "And, our college was a lot cheaper—less expensive. Maybe college is bigger today—more expectations. I don't know. I do know that Tonyae wants to get good grades in a good undergraduate program that will prepare her to get into medical school. She is so focused, so driven. And, she wants to go to a school with a great football team." Both friends laughed.

Both women had much to think about and challenges ahead. Leslie was invigorated to step up to her role as a board of trustee member, and she needed to engage with Chrissey in finding the right college. LaShonda had a similar challenge with helping Tonyae find the best fit for college. She had another professional challenge ahead, though—one that she wasn't ready to tell even her best friend.

NOTES

1. Jeffrey Satinover, *The Quantum Brain: The Search for Freedom and the Next Generation of Man* (New York: John Wiley & Sons, 2002), 6.

Bruce Lipton added to this notion, "Biology's most cherished tenets regarding genetic determinism are fundamentally flawed."

Lipton, *The Biology of Belief*, xiv.

2. Roland Omnes, *Quantum Philosophy: Understanding and Interpreting Contemporary Science* (Princeton, NJ: Princeton University Press, 1999), 81 and 82.

3. Wheatley, *Leadership and the New Science*, 169.

Wheatley further added:

Here is the real world described by new science. It is a world of interconnected networks. . . . In this highly sensitive system, the most minute actions can blow up into massive disruptions and chaos. . . . When chaos erupts, it not only disintegrates the current structure, it also creates the conditions for new order to emerge. . . . This is a world that knows how to organize itself without command, control, and charisma. . . . Self-organizing evokes creativity and results, creating strong, adaptive systems. Surprising new strengths and capacities emerge (170).

4. Capra, *The Tao of Physics*, 90.

Capra clarified: "In the new paradigm, we think that process is primary, that every structure we observe is a manifestation of an underlying process" (89).

5. Michael Talbot, *The Holographic Universe: The Revolutionary Theory of Reality* (New York: Harper Collins, 2011), 49.

6. Cole, *The Hole in the Universe*, 70.

Dr. Cole added, "The upshot was that Faraday took empty space and folded it with an interlocking network of permanent-press creases that connect everything in the universe to everything else—including matter and force" (72).

7. Einstein, *The Theory of Relativity*, 5.

Einstein further noted, "Physics deals with 'events in space and time.' To each event belongs, besides its place coordinates x, y, z, a time value of t" (6).

Not only is the observer's perception relative to their motion, but their view could be distorted. "Just as the warped or curved mirrors in an amusement park funhouse distort the normal spatial relationship of your reflection [the view caused by gravity is warped]."

Brian Greene, *The Elegant Universe: Superstrings, Hidden Dimensions, and the Quest for the Ultimate Theory* (New York: Vintage Books, 2000), 64.

8. Omnes, *Quantum Philosophy*, 129.

Omnes then more fully explained:

the special theory of relativity discovered by Einstein in 1905; space and time lose the absolute character they had always enjoyed in everyone's mind . . . distance and the passing of time depend on the motion of the observer measuring them. . . . [Einstein's theory of gravitational relativity then says]: not only do space and time become intimately connected as a result of motion but together they form a new entity, space-time [a fourth dimension], totally inaccessible to intuition and, moreover, having a curvature (125).

9. Capra, *The Tao of Physics*, 63.
10. Capra, *The Tao of Physics*, 208.
11. Cole, *The Hole in the Universe*, 126.
12. Greene, *The Elegant Universe*, 108.
13. Capra, *The Tao of Physics*, 54.

Capra further explained, "The revolution in modern physics foreshadowed an imminent revolution in biology, medicine, psychology, and economics, as well as a transformation of our world view and values. . . . including chaos and complexity theory (6).

14. Satinover, *The Quantum Brain*, 7.
15. Satinover, *The Quantum Brain*, 196.
16. Rettig, *Quantum Leaps in School Leadership*.

Much of the descriptive portions of this chapter have been borrowed from my earlier book, as described herein.

17. Fritjof Capra, *The Web of Life: A New Scientific Understanding of Living Systems* (New York: Anchor Books Doubleday, 1996), 31.
18. Michio Kaku, *Visions: How Science Will Revolutionize the 21st Century* (New York: Bantam Doubleday Dell Publishers, 1997), 107.
19. Satinover, *The Quantum Brain*, 127.
20. Shimon Malin, *Nature Loves to Hide: Quantum Physics and the Nature of Reality, a Western Perspective* (Oxford, United Kingdom: Oxford University Press, 2001), 237.

He explained:

He [Bohr] accepted the fact that what can be known about a quantum entity, such as an electron or an atom, cannot be contained in a single description. At least two seemingly contradictory descriptions are needed. The two descriptions are really complementary, rather than contradictory, because they apply to different circumstances. Each expresses an aspect of the truth; neither conveys the whole truth. The truth lies in the abyss between them and can be comprehended experientially to the extent that one can hold in one's mind, simultaneously, both descriptions, as well as the different circumstances in which they apply.

Bruce Lipton extended this concept to biology: "[E]very protein in our bodies is a physical/electromagnetic complement to something in the environment."

Lipton, *The Biology of Belief*, 159.
21. Capra, *The Web of Life*, 214–215.
22. Capra, *The Web of Life*, 145.
23. Omnes, *Quantum Philosophy*, 222.
24. Capra and Luisi, *Systems View of Life*, 73.
25. Wheatley, *Leadership and the New Science*, 35.

The impact of the observer is so central to quantum theory, that: "John Wheeler sees this involvement of the observer as the most important feature of quantum theory and he has therefore suggested replacing the word 'observer' with the word 'participator.'"

Capra, *The Web of Life*, 141.
26. Gary Zukav, *The Dancing Wu Li Masters: An Overview of the New Physics* (New York: Bantam, 1980), 111.
27. Gary Taubes, "Schizophrenic Atom Doubles as Schrodinger's Cat—or Kitten," *Science*, (May 1996), 1101.
28. Philip Yam, "Bringing Schrodinger's Cat to Life," *Scientific American*, (June 1997), 124.
29. Zukav, *The Dancing Wu Li Masters*, 293.
30. David Nield, "Physicists Just Achieved the First-Ever Quantum Teleportation Between Computer Chips," *Science Alert*, (December 31, 2019).
31. Satinover, *The Quantum Brain*, 184.
32. Omnes *Quantum Philosophy*, 229.
33. David Nield, "Scientists have Demonstrated Quantum Entanglement on a Tiny Satellite Orbiting Earth," *Science Alert* (June 28, 2020).
34. Talbot, *The Holographic Universe*, 79.
35. Talbot, *The Holographic Universe*, 33.
36. Capra, *The Web of Life*, 313.

He further noted: "The whole universe appears as a dynamic web of inseparable energy patterns. . . . They show that the properties of a particle can only be understood in terms of its activity—of its interactions with the surrounding environment. . . . In modern physics, the universe is thus experienced as a dynamic, inseparable whole which always incudes the observer in an essential way. In this experience, the traditional concepts of space and time, of isolated objects, and of cause and effect, lose their meaning" (80 and 81).

"The way in which they are connected—or *entangled*—is a very subtle thing."

Roger Penrose, *The Large, the Small, and the Human Mind* (Cambridge, United Kingdom: Cambridge University Press, 1997), 66.
37. Mihalyi Csikzentmihalyi, *Finding Flow: The Psychology of Engagement with Everyday Life* (New York: Basic Books, 1997), 141.

Professor Csikzentmihalyi went further, "Each of us is responsible for one particular point in space and time in which our body and mind forms a link within the total network of existence . . . we can make choices that will determine the future shape of the network of which we are a part" (146).

38. Joseph Jaworski, *Synchronicity: The Inner Path of Leadership* (San Francisco: Berrett-Koehler, 1996), 79.

39. Wheatley, *Leadership and the New Science*, 10.

40. Talbot, *The Holographic Universe*, 38.

41. Talbot, *The Holographic Universe*, 51.

This metaphor should not be too difficult to understand. We look out at a lake and may see a flat surface, not seeing the dynamic living system underneath. Intuitively we know what's out there, but we don't see it.

42. Malin, *Nature Loves to Hide*, 87.

43. Capra, *The Tao of Physics*, 223.

44. Cole, *The Hole in the Universe*.

45. Thomas Sergiovanni, *Value-Added Leadership: How to get Extraordinary Performance in Schools* (New York: Harcourt Brace Jovanovich Publishers, 1990), 44.

46. Jaworski, *Synchronicity*, 151.

47. Diane Fassel, "Lives in the Balance: The Challenge of Servant-Leaders in a Workaholic Society," In *Insights on Leadership: Service, Stewardship, Spirit, and Servant Leadership*, ed. L. Spears (New York: John Wiley & Sons, 1998), 218.

48. Senge, *The Fifth Discipline*, 168.

49. N. Champawat, "Sarvepalli Radhakrishnan" In *Great Thinkers of the Eastern World*, ed. Ian McGreal (New York: HarperCollins, 1995), 279.

50. Jaworski, *Synchronicity*, 57.

51. Ronald Pine, *Science and the Human Prospect* (Belmont, CA: Wadsworth, 2000), 245.

52. Capra, *The Web of Life*, 35.

53. Wheatley, *Leadership and the New Science*, 12.

54. Patrick Dolan, *Restructuring Our Schools: A Primer on Systemic Change* (Kansas City: Systems & Organization, 1994), 63.

55. Satinover, *The Quantum Brain*, 224.

Chapter 3

A Butterfly Spreads Her Wings

"The largely unconscious embrace of the mechanistic approach to management has now become one of the main obstacles to organizational change."[1]

On the other hand . . .

"I have come to believe that the new paradigm in science . . . has found its most appropriate formulation in the now emerging theory of living, self-organizing systems . . . It is a theory that applies to individual living organisms, social systems, and ecosystems."[2]

The literature is replete with evidence that our organizations behave more as ecosystems than as machines,[3] and this natural concept is equally applicable to our institutions of higher learning.[4] "This new conception of life involves a new kind of thinking—thinking in terms of relationships, patterns, and context. In science, this way of thinking is known as . . . 'systems thinking.'"[5] The present chapter will focus on lessons which can be gleaned from the natural sciences and applied directly to our natural human organizations such as our institutions of higher education.[6]

KEYSTONE SPECIES

While organizational theorists use a pyramid model to depict a system's structure, ecologists may also use a pyramid model showing plants as the base of the pyramid, predators on the top, and plant-eaters in the middle (see figure 3.1). In higher education, organizational theorists denote this pyramid model with students at the bottom, senior leadership at the top, and faculty and staff in the middle (see figure 3.2).

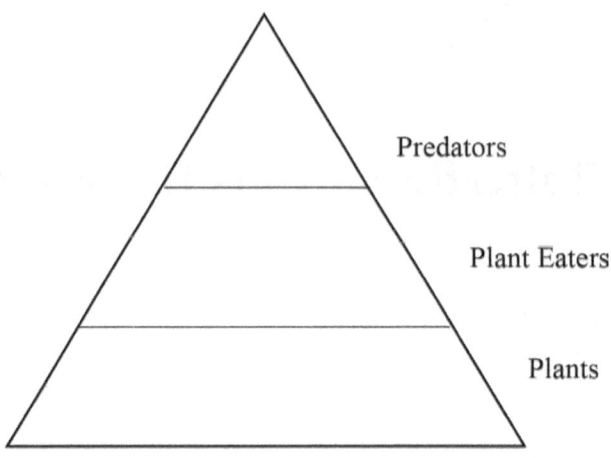

Figure 3.1 Ecological Pyramid Model. *Source*: Copyright Permission is not necessary.

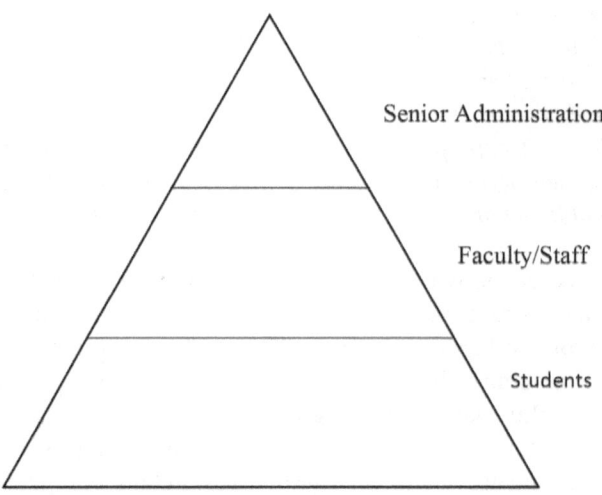

Figure 3.2 Higher Education Organizational Pyramid Model. *Source*: Copyright Permission is not necessary.

While the parallels may not be clean—students and plant-eaters, and senior administrators and predators (are qualitatively different thankfully), the overall schema remains the same. In October 2019, the Public Broadcast System (PBS) premiered, "The Serengeti Rules" on its *Nature* show. The program was based on the book of the same title by Sean B. Carroll (2017).[7]

"The Serengeti Rules" explored the emerging concept of "Keystone Species." The father of this concept was Dr. Bob Paine, a zoologist as the University of Washington. He noticed that by completely removing the predatory starfish from a protected ecosystem—a tidal pool—the mussels (plant-eaters) took over and destroyed all the plant-life since no predators were there to keep them in check.

So, rather than looking at the pyramid from the bottom-up, he saw that removing the predator, the top of the pyramid, had the largest impact on the ecosystem. Removal of other layers in the pyramid did not have the same devastating impact on the system. Thus, Paine discovered that some species are more important than others; he coined these species, "Keystone Predators."

Subsequent scientists found similar results and even extended this research's findings. Jim Estes of the University of California-Santa Cruz found similar results with sea otters, and in Oklahoma Mary Power—a freshwater ecologist—replicated these findings in rivers. She also noted that some predators keep prey in check with fear, so they are always on the move allowing for stable feeding patterns.

Duke University professor, Dr. John Terborgh, extended this research to mammals in the jungles of Venezuela. He coined the term, "downgrading" to explain the phenomenon of eliminating a Keystone Predator and the term, "upgrading" to describe the phenomenon of reintroducing a Keystone Predator to the ecosystem. Upgrading allowed the system to reset by creating a check on the system allowing for equilibrium or homeostasis.

The metaphor struggles a bit, here. Are we saying that those at the top of the pyramid are the keystones of the system? Are senior administrators more important than the faculty—those who are central to the mission of the institution? Are they more important than the students without whom the organization would not even exist? But, the research was not finished.

This body of research saw a profound shift under the work of Dr. Tony Sinclair, a zoologist with the University of British Columbia. He studied ecosystems in the Serengeti of East Africa. He found that significant reduction of wildebeests—plant-eaters—made the greatest negative impact on the ecosystem. This caused predators to die off, as well as overpopulation of grasses. Therefore, predators were not the Keystone, but rather plant-eaters were the Keystone. He thus coined the term, "Keystone Species to explain this phenomenon."

This research suggests that any layer in the ecosystem pyramid could be the Keystone—the most critical layer of the pyramid. Extending this lesson to the higher education organization metaphor that would suggest any layer may be the Keystone. Still, could we say that the faculty is more important than our students, or that students are more important than faculty, staff, and administration? The metaphor is strained, here.

Perhaps there are not Keystone *Species* but rather Keystone *Processes*. Rather than say a particular species is the critical *species* of an ecosystem, maybe a *process* is the critical aspect. For example, perhaps the process of renewal is the critical aspect of a natural ecosystem. Nature always seeks a state of equilibrium, or homeostasis. In order for homeostasis to exist, the system continually balancing each layer against the others. If one layer or level sees significant declines, the other levels get too large, and the system ultimately fails and dies.

Now the metaphor works for higher education organizational structure. Rather than looking for a critical layer in the pyramid, we should look for a critical process—a process that creates a system of checks and balances. In colleges and university settings, that system which best ensures checks and balances is shared governance. Both the natural ecosystem and the higher educational organization system process for checks and balances are depicted in figures 3.3 and 3.4 below.

When the system of checks and balances, provided by shared governance, is disrupted, the entire system becomes fragile and weakens. Shared governance provides each layer in the organization the place and opportunity to voice its concerns and ideas, keeping the other layers in check. Remove faculty authority or student voice, and senior administration may grow too strong for the system and result ultimately in a weakened institution.

Indeed, we have seen the slow and continued degradation of shared governance in higher education.[8] Over time, faculty has seen their authority abridged by an ever-increasing powerful executive while at the same time witnessing the corporatization of their governing boards of trustees.

Without faculty checking the authority of their administration, the institution is weakened. There then comes a tendency for external groups to dictate the curriculum, the mode of instruction, and perhaps even the quality of students. This change makes the health of the system untenable. Students may

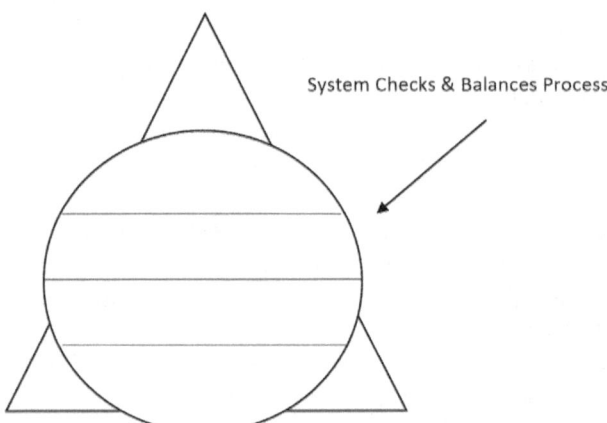

Figure 3.3 Ecological Pyramid Model with Checks & Balances. *Source*: Copyright Permission is not necessary

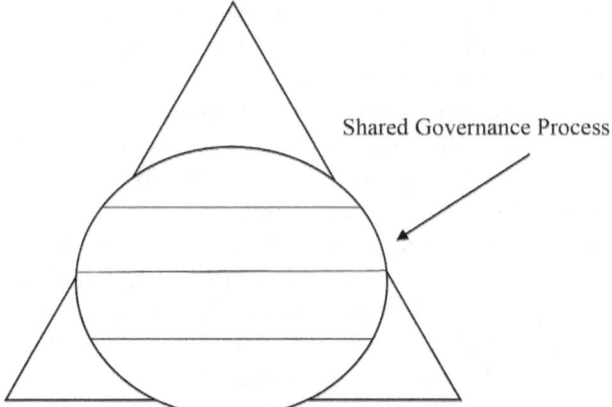

Figure 3.4 Higher Education Organizational Pyramid Model with Checks & Balances.
Source: Copyright Permission is not necessary

see less quality in instruction and expectations, and faculty becomes the hired hands of those making the unilateral decisions.

On the other hand, a too powerful faculty governance model will potentially seek stasis in an environment needing to change and adapt for survival. In this sense, faculty can deliberate the system to a slow death. Too much emphasis on student wants and students as customers can find an organization chasing new trends, seeking the lowest common denominator, and losing its original focus. Again, a system of shared governance checking and balancing each layer keeps the institution fit and adaptable.

CHAOS THEORY AND THE SCIENCE OF COMPLEXITY

When most of us went to school we learned that in classical thermodynamics a system's optimal level is equilibrium. In other words, all systems strive for equilibrium or homeostasis. This is how we have structured our organizations—to maintain order, stasis. We wish to maintain consistency and control where everything is at a state of equilibrium. Leaders hire managers to manage the system—to keep it under control.

In the previous discussion, we acknowledged that natural systems seek homeostasis. There are times, however, where this natural inclination can lead to death of the system. For example, should the environment make a dramatic shift (e.g., climate change), the natural inclination toward homeostasis can keep the system from adapting and making necessary changes for survival. In such cases, systems which can adapt will continue. Those that cannot will not survive.

In chaos theory (also known as dynamic systems theory) we learn that equilibrium is a state of entropy—the state where systems begin to die. When a system is at equilibrium, it cannot change, it begins to move toward entropy, and it dies. But when a system fluctuates and makes changes with its environment, it *appears* to be in disorder or in chaos. Yet, Capra posited, "In the new science of complexity, which takes its inspiration form the web of life, we learn that nonequilibrium is a source of order."[9]

The apex where the situation or experiment may either fall into true and total disarray or evolve into a higher level of order is called the bifurcation point. This is the point at which the system will either die or reorganize into a more robust and complex system. This happens in the lab, in nature, and in open systems. The following is an excellent laboratory example borrowed from Gary Zukav in *The Dancing Wu Li Masters*:[10]

> Imagine a large hollow cylinder into which is placed a smaller cylinder. The space between . . . is filled with a clear viscous liquid like glycerine (such a devise actually exists). Now suppose that we deposit a small droplet of ink on the surface of the glycerine. Because of the nature of the glycerine, the ink drop remains intact, a well-defined black spot floating on a clear liquid. (See figure 3.5)

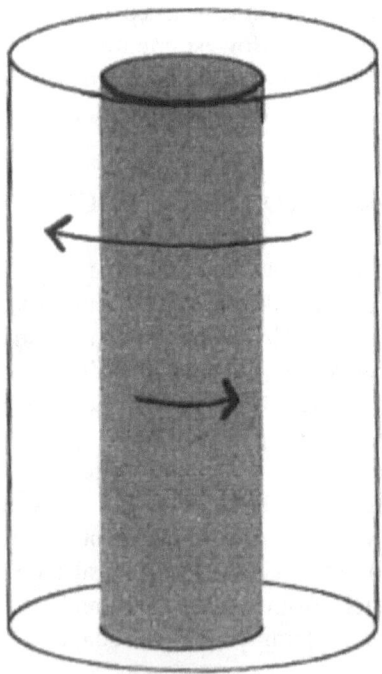

Figure 3.5 Glycerin Experiment. *Source*: Copyright Permission is not necessary

If we begin to rotate one of the cylinders, say in a clockwise direction, the drop of ink spreads out in the opposite direction, making a line which grows thinner and thinner until it disappears altogether. The ink droplet now is enfolded completely into the glycerine, *but it is still there.* When we rotate the cylinder in the opposite direction, the ink droplet reappears. A fine line appears which grows thicker and thicker and then collects into a single point. If we continue the counterclockwise notion of the cylinder, the same thing happens, but in reverse. We can repeat this process as often as we like.

While an example of bifurcation is easy to illustrate in the laboratory, other examples of bifurcation exist in our social systems. The fall of communism in the former Soviet Union is just such an example. The civil rights movement and the social upheaval of the Vietnam War are still other examples in our own nation's history. Higher education is currently seeing unmistakable signs of bifurcation and chaos as we move farther and farther from equilibrium. The signs include dozens of college campuses closing, the movement toward online degrees, MOOCs, and serious restrictions of financial support coupled with student loan indebtedness.

As has been mentioned earlier in this book, human organizations are not closed systems like machines. Rather, they are open systems. Natural systems always move away from equilibrium as they seek innovation. Innovation and creativity are the only way they can survive—they must adapt. "Chaos is ubiquitous in natural systems."[11]

What's more, "We now know that far from equilibrium, new types of structures may originate spontaneously. In far-from-equilibrium conditions we may have transformation from disorder, from thermal chaos, into order."[12] Chemists and physicists Prigogine and Stengers were explaining that what might appear to be disorder or chaos really has an underlying order. What the observer or organization's leader needs to do is allow for the order to appear.

Margaret Wheatley explained, "As chaos theory shows, if we look at such a system long enough and with the perspective of time, it always demonstrates its inherent orderliness."[13] We humans are only able to see a small portion of the system in terms of time and space across the organization. We do not see the system working in its entirety. We are not trained to do so.

Nonequilibrium is actually a source of order. As Prigogine and Stengers so eloquently stated:

In many cases it is difficult to disentangle the meaning of words such as "order" and "chaos." Is a tropical forest an ordered or chaotic system? The history of any particular animal species will appear very contingent, dependent on other species and on environmental accidents. Nevertheless, the feeling persists that, as such, the overall pattern of a tropical forest, as represented, for instance, by the diversity of species, corresponds to the very archetype of order.[14]

The science of complexity has taken the next logical step beyond chaos theory and has been applied to evolution, ecology, biology, computer science, and economics.[15] This science talks about interweaving relationships and networks, and about equilibrium as a sure sign of death.

The Santa Fe Institute in New Mexico is a fluid think-tank of some of the most brilliant minds in the world in physics, in economics, in politics, and in other fields. The scientists in the social fields know that their sciences cannot be reduced to simple linear formulas as done in the past. They know that real life is far too complex for such simplistic thinking. In his writings for real-life application of the science of complexity, Michael Waldrop explained, "These complex, self-organizing systems are *adaptive*. . . . Species evolve for better survival in a changing environment—and so do corporations and industries."[16] Economic professor at Stanford University Brian Arthur extrapolated on this natural concept—as cited by Waldrop:

> Conventional economics, the kind he'd been taught in school, was about as far from this vision of complexity as you could imagine. Theoretical economists endlessly talked about the stability of the marketplace, and the balance of supply and demand. They transcribed the concept of mathematical equations and proved theorems about it. . . . But Arthur had embraced instability. . . . Like it or not, the market-place isn't stable. The *world* isn't stable. It's full of evolution, upheaval, and surprise.[17]

The Santa Fe Institute has closely analyzed the science of complexity and the lessons that can be learned from chemistry, quantum physics, and molecular biology and how these lessons can be applied to complex organizations and systems. Capra and Luisi describe characteristics of biological life[18]—which have parallels to organizations. Molecular biologist Horace Freeland Judson posited, "The real economy was not a machine but a kind of living system, with all the spontaneity and complexity . . . in the world of molecular biology."[19] Waldrop went on to cite the work of John Holland, computer scientist at the University of Michigan. In Waldrop's words:

> Holland started by pointing out that the economy is an example of "complex adaptive systems." In the natural world systems include brains, immune systems, ecologies, cells, developing embryos, and ant colonies. In the human world, they included cultural and social systems such as political parties or scientific communities.[20]

Again, Waldrop reported on the scientific work of scientists—this time of Los Alamos physicist Doyne Farmer who talked of how the former Soviet Union changed at the edge of chaos as did the big three American auto-makers because of the competition coming from Japan. Farmer stated, "Common sense, not to mention recent political experience, suggests that healthy economies and healthy societies alike have to keep order and chaos in balance. . . . They leave plenty of room for creativity, change, and respond to new conditions."[21] Clearly, administrators choosing to tightly control their organizations in tough times may actually be squeezing the life out of their systems—a very ironic twist.

Waldrop shared one final real-life example of complexity science in action. "In the fossil record, says [biologist Stuart Kauffman of the University of Pennsylvania], this process would show up as long periods of stasis followed by bursts of evolutionary change—exactly the kind of 'punctuated equilibrium' that many paleontologists, notably Stephen J. Gould, and Niles Eldridge, claim that they do see in the record."[22] So, change can happen slowly and incrementally over time, or change can happen abruptly in an instant—like a tornado or fire. In a university an academic department may slowly adapt its curriculum, or abruptly change to a new delivery method, for example, online instruction.

There are three primary lessons we can take from chaos theory and the science of complexity back to the people in our organizations. First, people need to be patient when things *appear* to be chaotic. We need to take the time to let patterns develop, and to look over the entire system for patterns or themes with respect to space and time. The term "space" refers to the entire organization. We must look beyond our own departments or silos to see the interconnections, networks, and relationships. The term "time" refers to taking more than the typical snapshot of time in which we make our observations and assessments, to look in terms of months or even years.

That's why so much of what we see appears to be chaotic. A glimpse of nearly anything can appear chaotic. But, over time, patterns or themes emerge and reveal themselves. So, if we look at the system over space and time, we are more likely to better understand the order embedded in the chaos—it's "chaotic." Stephen Covey embraces apparent chaos: "As a teacher, I have come to believe that many truly great classes teeter on the edge of chaos. There are times when neither the teacher nor the student knows for sure what's going to happen."[23]

The second lesson teaches us that change and adaptation to the environment must happen in order for a system to survive. Organizations need to move, at times, from equilibrium in order to create and to grow to a higher level of complexity. Without such change, far from equilibrium, the system will die.

The third lesson from chaos theory and the science of complexity is no less important. "A small fluctuation may start an entirely new evolution that will drastically change the whole behavior of the macroscopic system. The analogy with social phenomena . . . is inescapable."[24] That is to say that most apparently insignificant issues can create major changes. In the science of meteorology this has become known as the "butterfly effect." In terms of human organizations, one person can indeed make an enormous impact—anywhere in the system.

DISSIPATIVE STRUCTURES AND CHEMICAL CLOCKS

Dissipative structures evolve within open systems. As Alvin Toffler wrote in the forward to Prigogine's and Stenger's book:

> While some parts of the universe may operate like machines, these are closed systems, and closed systems, at best, form only a small part of the physical universe. Most phenomenon of interest to us are, in fact, *open* systems, exchanging energy or matter (and one might add, information) with their environment. Surely biological and social systems are open, which means that the attempt to understand them in mechanistic terms is doomed to failure. This suggests, moreover, that most of reality, instead of being orderly, stable, and equilibrial, is seething and bubbling with change, disorder, and process.[25]

Therefore, open systems can only survive when they change by adapting to their environment. Since human systems and their organizations are open systems, change is crucial to their survival. We must allow for disorder and apparent chaos to work. Dissipative structures, as we shall soon see, emerge from open systems and can continue to live only through the process of change. These systems actually actively seek change.

The term "dissipative structures" was innovated by Ilya Prigogine. It refers to the concept that open systems maintain features of both change and stability. In fact, change is what allows stability. In other words, order does indeed come out of chaos. In order to survive, a natural system leaps into an apparent chaos. In complexity sciences, the fine line between order or equilibrium and chaos is where change and renewed life occurs.

Nobel laureate Ilya Prigogine himself and coauthor Isabelle Stengers wrote: "One of the most interesting aspects of dissipative structures is their coherence. The system behaves as a whole, as if it were the site of long-range forces. . . . The system is structured as though each molecule were 'informed' about the overall state of the system."[26]

Before Prigogine studied the more complex systems of living organisms, he developed his theory of dissipative structures by learning of the "Benard instability," named after the French physicist Henri Benard. Fritjof Capra explained:

Henri Benard discovered that the heating of a thin layer of liquid may result in strangely ordered structures. When the liquid is uniformly heated below, a constant heat flux is established, moving from the bottom to the top. The liquid itself remains at rest, and the heat is transferred by conduction alone. However, when the temperature difference between the top and bottom surfaces reach a certain critical value, the heat flux is replaced by heat convection, in which the heat is transferred by coherent motion of large numbers of molecules.

At this point a very striking ordered pattern of hexagonal (honeycomb) cells appears, in which hot liquid rises through the center of the cells, while the cooler liquid descends to the bottom along the cell walls. Prigogine's detailed analysis of these "Benard cells" showed that as a system moves farther away from equilibrium (that is, from a state with uniform temperature throughout the liquid), it reaches a critical point of instability, at which the ordered hexagonal pattern emerges.[27] (See figure 3.6)

What Benard, Prigogine and Stengers, and Capra showed us is that while open systems may appear to be disorganized, there is some underlying organization and communication going on; we just can't see it. As the system moves further and further away from equilibrium or stability, it will finally reach a point of coherence and newfound stability.

Figure 3.6 Dissipative Structure—Benard Cells. *Source*: https://psl.noaa.gov/outreach/education/science/convection/img/

Again, as with the inherent communication of molecules at macroscopic distances as described in the previous chapter on quantum physics, communication is critical to open systems as described by chemists. (The reader is reminded of Bell's Theorem or nonlocal causality where two atoms are separated at long distances but are somehow able to communicate instantaneously over time and space). Somehow, there is communication among those interrelated parts. Or, *perhaps they are not as separate as they appear*.

Prigogine cited another naturally occurring example of dissipative structures in open systems—the vortex tunnel, such as whirlpools and tornadoes. These temporary systems appear to be highly chaotic, but in truth, they are highly organized with an internal structure. The initial instability accelerates and soon self-organizes and emerges as the funnel-shape we all recognize.

> This continuing acceleration [in a whirlpool] ends not in catastrophe but in a new stable state. At a certain rotational speed, centrifugal forces come into play that push the water radially away from the drain. Thus, the water surface above the drain develops a depression, which quickly turns into a funnel. Eventually, a miniature tornado of air forms inside this funnel, creating highly complex and nonlinear structures . . . inside the vortex.
>
> In the end the force of gravity pulling the water down the drain and the water pressure pushing outward balance each other and result in a stable state . . . The acting forces [gravity and friction] are now interlinked in self-balancing feedback loops that give great stability to the vortex structure as a whole.[28]

Again, we are shown that somehow the seemingly disorganized and chaotic system self-organizes and a new order comes into existence. The message from dissipative structures is clear. As Margaret Wheatley so eloquently puts it:

> Dissipative structures demonstrate that *disorder* can be a source of *order*, and that most growth is found in disequilibrium, not in balance. The things we fear most in organizations—fluctuations, disturbances, imbalances—need not be signs of an impending disorder that will destroy us. Instead, fluctuations are the primary source of creativity.[29]

Chemical clocks prove to be another amazing dissipative structure phenomenon that provide intriguing insights into systems. For one final time, we turn to Fritjof Capra for this excellent description:

> [Chemical clocks show] reactions far from equilibrium, which produce very striking periodic oscillations. For example, if there are two kinds of molecules

in the reaction, one "red" and one "blue," the system will be all blue at a certain point; then change its color abruptly to red; then again to blue; and so on at regular intervals—like clockwork. Different experimental conditions may also produce waves of chemical activity.

> To change all at once, the chemical system has to act as a whole, producing a high degree of order through the coherent activity of billions of molecules. Prigogine and his colleagues discovered that, as in the Benard convection, this coherent behavior emerges spontaneously at critical points of instability far from equilibrium.[30]

Prigogine himself wrote that "in chemistry the relation between order and chaos appears highly complex; successive regimes of ordered (oscillatory) situations follow regimes of chaotic behavior."[31] Again, as with quantum physics' nonlocal causality, and as with chemistry's dissipative structures, molecules show a sense of relationships and corresponding communication that seems counterintuitive to our Western linear minds. In Prigogine's concluding note:

> Particles separated by macroscopic distances become linked. Local events have repercussions throughout the whole system. . . . Nonequilibrium is a source of order. Here the situation is especially clear. At equilibrium molecules behave as essentially independent entities; they ignore one another. We would like to call them "hypnons," "sleepwalkers." Though each of them may be as complex as we like, they ignore one another. However, nonequilibrium wakes them up and introduces a coherence quite foreign to equilibrium.[32]

Could hypnons or sleepwalkers exist in our own organizations? What form of nonequilibrium would need to wake them up? The message from these experiments and from nature itself must be clear to institutional leaders. Communication is central to the revitalization and survival of open systems. Furthermore, again, what might appear to be chaos, is either order that we have not taken the time or breadth of view to see or is part of the process of the system attempting to renew itself. We need to allow or encourage this process to occur.

In a most fascinating view of natural system collectivity, Lipton describes the process of natural cellular community adaptation:

> Living organisms, it turns out, actually integrate their cellular communities by sharing their genes. . . . [G]enes are shared not only among the individual members of a species but also among members of different species. The sharing of genetic information via gene transfer speeds up evolution since organisms

can acquire "learned" experiences from other organisms. Given this sharing of genes, organisms can no longer be seen as disconnected entities; there is no wall between species.[33]

However, our organizational systems aren't built for adaptability; they are built to maintain consistency and control. We aren't trained to look at the entirety of the system—only the parts and data points. We don't look at it contextually over space and time. We are trained to control and hold tightly to information and communication. We don't have systems of checks and balances. Rather we use top-down decision making in order to manage and to keep change from occurring. In other words, our practice, in practical terms, is to kill our organizations.

LESSONS LEARNED

Several quick lessons can be learned from a study of the newer sciences. They fit very cleanly with the lessons we have learned from quantum physics; in fact, they support, complement, and reinforce those lessons and will give direction toward organizational application.

- Organizations are like living natural systems.
- Communication is the life blood of an organization.[34]
- Systems need a process of internal checks to keep the whole in balance.
- In order for systems to live they must adapt, change, and create.[35]
- Equilibrium may be the sign of death of a system; disequilibrium can create renewal and life.
- Control might squeeze life out of the system.
- What might appear to be chaos might actually be in order. Indeed, sometimes order comes from chaos.
- Change can be slow and incremental, or it can be abrupt and punctuated.
- Small perturbations or disturbances can have a huge influence anywhere in the system.
- Must look at the system as a whole, over time and space.
- Communication with feedback loops across the system is critical.

In a fitting conclusion to this section of the chapter, we end with the words of Dr. Csikszentmihalyi:

> *Darwin's observations . . . the idea that over very long periods of time ecological systems and the structure of organisms tend toward increasing complexity has given hope to several scientists that the universe is not ruled by chaos but conceals a meaningful story.*[36]

With those words of wisdom, let us now turn to the stories of an existing practitioner—Dr. Joe Dennis—and then to our protagonist Leslie.

ESSAY—JOE DENNIS

My work in higher education spans two decades and has been primarily focused in mass communication, both as a practitioner (sports information director, public service associate) and as an educator (instructor, professor). I worked at three different institutions, one large public institution and two small private colleges. I have worked under nine direct supervisors, five academic deans, six vice presidents and four college presidents.

Trying to please a plethora of bosses—direct and indirect, and sometimes with different objectives—has been quite challenging. In his landmark 2000 *Harvard Business Review* study, "Leadership That Gets Results," emotional intelligence guru Daniel Goleman identifies six leadership styles: the pacesetter, authoritative, affiliative, coaching, coercive and democratic.[37] I witnessed leadership from each category, each producing different results. *(Note: names have been changed to protect the identity of those still in the field.)*

The Pacesetting Leader

Summed up, the modus operandi of the pacesetting leader is to "set high standards for performance," and the phrase that best sums up this leader is, "Do as I do, now."

I worked under this dean for three highly productive, yet exhausting years as a staff member. I was very excited when I learned Kathryn would be my boss, due to her high record of accomplishment at her previous institution. And she hit the ground running, instituting many changes that benefitted both faculty and staff. One of them was stripping away middle management, giving her direct supervision to many employees, including me. She was not above doing anything. I'll never forget how after a college-wide event, she stuck behind to help staff pick up chairs and straighten the room. That small action meant so much to so many people.

We all had access to direct access to Kathryn, it was not unusual to get texts or emails from her in the middle of the night. She was 100 percent committed to her job, and expected the same of us. And it was evident that this leadership style was praised from above, as long-awaited capital projects that required administrative support were finally being completed . . . at a rapid pace. This quick rate of change frustrated many faculty members, some noting that if your thoughts didn't align with Kathryn's vision, you were shut out of the conversation.

Personally, I had high admiration for Kathryn and how she was able to get things accomplished. I bought into her vision and was a fierce defender for her. It was my wife who recognized just how exhausting my new boss was making me. For example, my busiest time of the year was April, May, and June, where I managed an annual awards competition for high school media, planned a journalism summer camp for high school students, and hosted a workshop for high school journalism teachers.

In February, Kathryn informed me that the college would be hosting a ten-day institute in May of that year and that I would be the perfect person to handle it, assuring me I would be compensated for the extra work. Raising three boys and caring for an ailing father, this was the last thing I wanted, regardless of the money.

Of course, I persisted and did my job to the fullest of my potential, but soon soured on Kathryn's leadership style, often avoiding her for fear more work would be added to my already packed agenda.

The Authoritative Leader

Goldman says the authoritative leader "mobilizes people toward a vision" and is best summed up with the phrase, "Come with me."

I worked under an authoritative leader for five years. Although not my direct supervisor, Bryan was dean and I was part of the team that met weekly with him. I admired Bryan's vision for the school, and he was an inspiring speaker using his vast knowledge of history to link the present to the future. His long career in academia and calming nature was the perfect antidote to our previous leader, who serving in an interim capacity, seemingly had no vision other than the bottom line.

However, I quickly recognized flaws in Bryan's leadership style. Although he communicated a vision that most agreed with, he failed to get input into how to get us there. He had some confidants in key positions who served as his "yes" men, and he ultimately pushed changes through making unilateral decisions. This angered many faculty members who felt like their expertise was being ignored. In one situation, Bryan invested millions in developing a TV station to fill a news void in the community.

Like most of his aspirations, the goal was admirable. It would serve the community and give our students a real-world teaching lab to develop skills. But the methods to get there were highly controversial. One prominent professor told me, "I spent my whole career buying and selling TV stations. But not one time did Bryan come to me for advice. He is going about this the wrong way."

Indeed, the project was mired in overhead expenses and the university ultimately pulled the plug on the station, losing millions of dollars in the process.

The Affiliative Leader

The affiliative leader "creates harmony and builds emotional bonds," and is best summed up with the phrase, "People come first."

My favorite direct supervisor was an affiliative leader who I worked under for six years. Stan was an awesome boss. He directed a team of six highly educated, competent, and opinionated individuals. Stan valued not only each team member's expertise, but also each of us as individuals. He would often inquire about my family and remember seemingly innocuous details of my personal life that I had shared. For example, in a late Tuesday afternoon meeting I'd say I have to leave by 4:30 to get my son to his baseball game. The next morning, Stan would ask, "How did the baseball game go?"

In terms of our work production, he was hands-off. He would often say, "You know what you were hired to do, and you know how to do it best." This doesn't mean he was indifferent to our work. He was always there to answer to questions or offer feedback, and he was happy to do it. What's most impressive about Stan is how he created a team atmosphere. We had monthly happy hours and would go out to lunch on each other's birthdays. This paid off in the work, because although we all had distinctly different jobs, we all chipped in to help out each other, and Stan would, too.

One frustration some of my colleagues stated about Stan's leadership style was that he did not try to push through major institutional changes that needed to happen for us as a team to be more effective. But I didn't share in that frustration. I think Stan recognized what was in the realm of possibility with the current leadership of the college, and chose to not waste energy starting battles he knew would likely not be won.

Others felt that Stan did not hold people accountable when they failed to perform to expectations. However, I think Stan chose to celebrate accomplishments publicly and critique people personally, so it gave the appearance people were not being held accountable.

The Coaching Leader

"Try this" is the motto of the coaching leader, whose main method involves "developing people for the future."

I was lucky to have a coaching leader as my boss for my first professional job in academia. I was replacing a long-time, highly respected and beloved sports information director at a small private college. My supervisor—the director of communications—took a chance on me when she hired me, and that skepticism was evident on the dozen or so coaches I would be working within the athletic department. But Barbara consistently showed her belief in me, offering constructive criticism of my work and tips on how to deal with coaches who were always there to point out every mistake I made.

One moment in particular that exemplifies her style was when I was struggling to get coverage of our athletic teams from a local newspaper that always covered our school when my predecessor was in charge. I knew coaches and administrators were frustrated. After confirming I was following the proper protocol to share information with the newspaper, Barbara made an appointment with the newspaper's editor and accompanied me on a visit. I knew Barbara always had my back, and I tried my hardest not to disappoint her. I wanted to make her look good.

Honestly, I don't know if I would thrive working under Barbara now. I would likely be bothered by her consistent feedback—just let me do my job! It was fate—she was the perfect boss for me at the perfect time.

The Coercive Leader

The coercive leader "demands immediate compliance" and can be best summed up with the phrase, "Do what I tell you." Not surprisingly, Goldman lists this type of leader as the least effective, as it easily destroys morale, stifles creativity and silences dissent.

I've been lucky to not have a coercive leader as a direct supervisor in higher education, but I have witnessed the damage it can do on an institutional level. I've found the best thing to do when such a leader exists at the top is to stay in my lane and hope the leader rarely enters it. And if he enters it too much, or if I see the institution's foundation crumbling, I need to start looking for another place to work.

The Democratic Leader

The modus operandi of the democratic leader is to "forge consensus through participation" and is summed up with the phrase, "What do you think?"

I had my first democratic leader supervisor when I entered the faculty ranks. This was truly evident at my first faculty meeting, when Stacy would provide an agenda and each of us would provide comment on each item. When decisions had to be made, we would vote, and if the vote was not unanimous, the dissenters would be asked why they were uncomfortable with the decision. Even on an individual level, when Stacy commented on my performance, it would always be approached in an empowering way rather than a command. Stacy would ask, "Have you considered doing this?" rather than say, "You should do this."

I truly appreciate this style of leadership. I felt respected and that my voice mattered—my education and expertise meant something! While this style works on a smaller level, I have seen how it fails at an institutional level.

I've been in democratically-led school faculty meetings where good ideas for change have been resisted by a few prominent faculty members, and "group-think" infiltrates more impressionable faculty. I've even felt betrayed by colleagues who privately told me they agreed with me, but when I mentioned it in a meeting they failed to back me up. Because the democratic leader relies on consensus, change can be difficult to attain. Even if everyone agrees change is necessary, building a consensus on how to get there can be impossible. Sometimes, the leader just needs to make a decision that will not satisfy everyone.

As a new department chair, I am finding myself implementing a combination of these leadership styles. I'm rooted in the democratic style, but I have learned to make decisions even if I cannot get everyone on board (I do make sure I have a majority, however). I've implemented the coaching style to a new faculty member who was not only new to the college, but new to teaching.

I've added elements of the affiliative leader by instituting annual Christmas and year-end outings, and publicly celebrating birthdays. I've incorporated some authoritative leadership by making budgetary decisions that automatically set the priorities of the department. And I've been known to be a pacesetter, sometimes overcommitting myself and my colleagues for the benefit of the overall department in the eyes of administration.

I recognize that my leadership style has many flaws, and it's a constantly evolving skill that often requires tinkering. Ultimately, I think that's the most important trait for leaders that is often not discussed. Leaders need to be vulnerable. Leaders need to apologize when they get it wrong. And leaders need to learn from their mistakes.

LESLIE'S LAMENT

LaShonda's "starter dough" business was her own creation. She began this endeavor at her home, and it blossomed fairly quickly. Within two years of its creation, she had a brick-and-mortar store with nearly a dozen employees, and a web presence that really drove her business. Within five years, her new company was so successful that she had four stores in three states employing over sixty people. Most orders came through her website. She was named entrepreneur of the year in her third year as Owner/President.

"Starter Over" had become so successful, it was taking too much of LaShonda's time. She had been quietly talking with a couple of her executive board members that she was thinking of stepping back from her president responsibilities and focus her energies as owner and chair of the board. She was getting some mixed feedback from her board leadership team.

LaShonda shared all this with her best friend, in confidence, at breakfast earlier this morning. Leslie wasn't quite sure how to respond, and she said as much. LaShonda's response was fully accepting. "That's okay, Leslie. I just wanted to share this with you. Your listening was all that I needed."

But presently, Leslie sat next to LaShonda at the Chamber of Commerce board of directors meeting. Leslie was her special guest. As a guest, Leslie spoke briefly about the local school district and the student demographic, in general terms. She spent the rest of the meeting absorbing the culture of the meeting, always filtering through the lens of her new experience as a college trustee.

The Chamber board meeting started with a roll call vote of members in attendance. All members had received a packet of materials, including the agenda and monthly financial statement, via their portal earlier in the week. After the roll call and call to order by the chamber chair, welcoming remarks were made by Bill Parmier—vice president of First State Bank. As each board meeting was held at a different location, the host this month—Mr. Parmier—was the perfect person to welcome the board members. He also sponsored a continental breakfast for everyone to enjoy.

The first action was approval of the minutes from the previous meeting, followed immediately by approval of the consent agenda. There was one minor change to the minutes; Millie Crenshaw noted an incorrect date with an upcoming event at the state capital. This was quickly rectified.

The next item took a bit more time—roughly fifteen minutes—approval of the month's financial statement. Treasurer August Willey quickly ran over the key routine points. However, he spent a few more moments explaining a discrepancy between this month's statement and the last. The concern had to do with a double entry of dues caused by a new software system upgrade. There were no problems, but revenues were actually nearly $3,000 less than previously reported. Still, according to August, the finances continued to be strong and overall revenues were up compared to last year point in time. The financial statement was approved without discussion.

Committee Reports took the next ten minutes of presentation and discussion. Mostly quick updates and announcements were made. A couple of the committee chairs had nothing to report. Such reporting actually seemed rather perfunctory to Leslie.

There were two items under Old Business: The first item focused on the role Chamber members wanted to take, as a body, in support of the upcoming referendum for an upgrade to the local hospital. The group was evenly split between those who wanted to remain neutral and not take a formal role, and those who said it was imperative to actively support this endeavor. Such an upgrade to these facilities, they reasoned, could only bring in new businesses and families. Board members were cordial, but their thoughts on both sides were firm and remained steadfast. Since no clear opinion took favor, no decision was made.

The second item under Old Business led to no discussion. Hector Villereal announced that he had now finalized membership for the Chamber committee on encouraging tourism in the county. The first meeting would be held Monday morning and would serve as a mini-strategic planning session. A special guest would present what her Chamber over in the neighboring state had done in similar efforts.

Under New Business, the only topic was preparations for the new class of Leadership Southbey. Mozul Khadameer, chair of the committee, provided an update to the board. No real discussion occurred, but there was great unanimity that this program was well worth the time and expense by identifying and helping the next generation of community leaders. A couple quick suggestions of improvements to the curriculum were discussed but no changes of significance.

The meeting concluded with the President's Report and a list of upcoming events for the month. The executive, Pauline Greene, was pretty brief in her remarks. She handed around two documents to each board member. The first document was a bulleted list describing recent activity of the Chamber, and the second list was a calendar of events.

Pauline encouraged all board members to attend as many events as their schedules would permit. She expressed a little disappointment in attendance at the recent Business after Hours events. She asked for ideas on how to increase attendance. No real ideas came forward—the overall sentiment was that people's schedules were too busy. Pauline noted the next meeting would focus on gathering momentum and ideas for the summer fundraising event—the annual LakeFest.

The chair asked for a motion to adjourn. LaShonda moved, and it was seconded by three people simultaneously. Leslie's overall impression was that this was collectively a very pleasant group of local professionals who deeply cared about their community. They received her warmly and were very, very interested in hearing about her students. A couple of board members came up to her afterwards and told her of recent graduates that they had hired. Leslie enjoyed her time with the Chamber this morning.

NOTES

1. Capra and Luisi, *Systems View of Life*, 59.
2. Capra, *The Tao of Physics*, 339.
3. Margaret Wheatley, *Leadership and the New Science: Learning about Organizations from an Orderly Universe* (San Francisco: Berrett-Koehler, 1994).
   Fritjof Capra, *The Hidden Connections: A Science of Sustainable Living* (New York: Anchor Books, 2004).

4. Rettig, *Quantum Leaps in School Leadership*.

5. Capra and Luisi, *Systems View of Life*, xii.

These two authors added: "A full understanding of biological phenomena is reached only when we approach it through the interplay of three different levels of description—the biology of the observed phenomena, the laws of physics and biochemistry, and the nonlinear dynamics of complex systems" (261). To which they added: "In spite of ongoing change, the organism maintains its overall identity or pattern of organization" (255).

6. Perry Rettig, "Shared Governance: The 'Keystone' Process to the Higher Education Ecology Survival," *The Academy for Advancing Leadership*, (December, 2019).

This section of chapter 3 is borrowed extensively from my article from AAL.

7. Sean B. Carroll, *The Serengeti Rules* (Princeton, NJ: Princeton University Press, 2016). "The Serengeti Rules." *Nature*. Video of the Public Broadcasting System. Edited by Benedict Jackson. Executive Producer: David Guy Elisco, Jared Lipworth, and Fred Kaufman. Produced by David Allen and Gaby Bastyra. October 9, 2019. Based on the book by Sean B. Carroll. (2016). *The Serengeti Rules*. Princeton, NJ: Princeton University Press.

8. Perry Rettig, *Shared Governance: A More Meaningful Approach in Higher Education* (Lanham, MD: Rowman & Littlefield, 2020).

9. Capra, *The Web of Life*, 190.

10. Zukav, *The Dancing Wu Li Masters*, 306–307.

11. Satinover, *The Quantum Brain*, 203.

12. Ilya Prigogine and Isabelle Stengers, *Order out of Chaos* (New York: Bantam Books, 1984), 307.

13. Wheatley, *Leadership and the New Science*, 21.

14. Prigogine and Stengers, *Order out of Chaos*, 169.

15. Satinover, *The Quantum Brain*, 204.

Bruce Lipton added: "The cell membrane was indeed a structural and functional equivalent (homologue) of a silicon chip! . . . B.A. Cornell and associates successfully turned a biological cell membrane into a digital read-out computer chip."

Lipton, *The Biology of Belief*, 61.

16. Michael Waldrop, *Complexity: The Emerging Science at the Edge of Order and Chaos* (New York: Simon & Schuster, 1992), 11.

17. Waldrop, *Complexity*, 17.

18. Capra and Luisi, *Systems View of Life*, 345–346.

These include:

A living system is materially and energetically open; it is a dissipative structure, operating far from equilibrium. There is a continual flow of energy and matter through the system.

It is self-organizing, its structure being organized by the system's own internal rules.

Its dynamics are nonlinear and may include the emergence of new order at critical points of instability.

It is operationally closed—an autopoietic, bounded network.

It is self-generating; each component helps to transform and replace other components including those of its semipermeable boundary.

Its interactions with the environment are cognitive—that is, determined by its own internal organization.

In such a system these authors add, "The web of life is a flexible, ever-fluctuating network. The more variables are kept fluctuating, the more dynamic is the system, the greater is its flexibility, and the great is its ability to adapt to changing conditions" (355).

19. Waldrop, *Complexity*, 31.
20. Waldrop, *Complexity*, 145.
21. Waldrop, *Complexity*, 294.
22. Waldrop, *Complexity*, 308.
23. Covey, *The Seven Habits*, 265.
24. Prigogine and Stengers, *Order out of Chaos*, 14.
25. Prigogine and Stengers, *Order out of Chaos*, xv.
26. Prigogine and Stengers, *Order out of Chaos*, 171.
27. Capra, *The Web of Life*, 86–87.
28. Capra, *The Web of Life*, 170.
29. Wheatley, *Leadership and the New Science*, 20.
30. Capra, *The Web of Life*, 88.
31. Prigogine and Stengers, *Order out of Chaos*, 168.
32. Prigogine and Stengers, *Order out of Chaos*, 180.
33. Lipton, *The Biology of Belief*, 14.
34. Wheatley, *Leadership and the New Science*.

Lipton added a note from communication in biology: "The function of the nervous system is to perceive the environment and coordinate the behavior of all the other cells in the vast cellular community."

Bruce Lipton, *The Biology of Belief: Unleashing the Power of Consciousness, Matter & Miracles* (New York: Hay House, 2008), 10.

35. Capra and Luisi, *The Systems View of Life*.

These authors further stipulated:

"Since the environment changes naturally, the likely result of the changes must have been that, in order to survive, the living species with time had to adapt and therefore change. Therefore the organisms must display *adaptation due to environmental changes*" (183).

36. Csikzentmihalyi, *Finding Flow*, 142–143.

An interesting aside—French biologist, Jean-Baptiste de Lamarck had a competing notion of evolution to that of Darwin. "Lamarck's theory suggested that evolution was based on 'instructive,' cooperative interaction among organisms and their environment that enables life forms to survive and evolve in a dynamic world."

Bruce Lipton, *The Biology of Belief: Unleashing the Power of Consciousness, Matter & Miracles* (New York: Hay House, 2008), 11.

37. Daniel Goleman. "Leadership that gets Results." *Harvard Business Review* 78(2), 2000: 78–90.

Chapter 4

Quantum Redux

"Ideas of space and time are part of the shaky foundation on which is balanced the whole intricate and beautiful structure of scientific theory and philosophical thought. To tamper with those ideas is to send a shudder from one end of the structure to another."

—*Banesh Hoffman*[1]

Indeed, the structure of scientific theory has changed, and we now feel the shudder. In chapter 2, we explored the sine qua non science of relativity theory and the subsequent foundational knowledge of quantum mechanics. We have learned that these sciences and their mathematics have changed our notions and understandings of not only physics, but biology and chemistry, computer technology, economics, and even social theory. A very intriguing yet inchoate picture is forming about the human brain as a quantum system, as well.

THE QUANTUM BRAIN

Not only may the brain be a quantum processor, but the entire body may be, too. "The view of the human body as a machine and of the mind as a separate entity is being replaced by one that sees not only the brain, but also the immune system, the bodily tissues, and even each cell a living, cognitive system."[2]

The human brain relies on dual aspects, process and structure.[3] In a most interesting description of our minds as functioning as real holographs, Michael Talbot noted, "Memories are distributed through the brain, not isolated to a part or neurons like originally proposed."[4] But, even more intriguing is the research by Candace Pert as described by Bruce Lipton: "Pert revealed how her study of information-processing receptors on nerve cell membranes led her to discover that the same 'neural' receptors were present on most, if not all, of the body's cells. Her elegant experiments established that the 'mind' was not focused in the head but was distributed via signal molecules to the whole body."[5]

The implications are staggering. The whole body keeps memories; the body thinks; the body communicates and has feedback loops. Like there is a particle-wave duality, and a space-time duality—one cannot be considered without the other, there is a brain-body duality or complementarity. Capra and Luisi described the work of American psychologist, William James, who extended this thinking by noting that "consciousness is . . . an ever-changing stream, and he emphasized the personal, continuous, and highly integrated nature of this stream of consciousness."[6]

The very notion of the extensive and expansive nature of mind-brain interconnectedness comes directly from quantum mechanics. In the words of physicist Roger Penrose, "Non-local effects like this occur in quantum mechanics and they cannot be understood in terms of one thing being separate from another—some sort of global activity is taking place."[7] Furthermore, the brain uses mathematical processes of probabilities to instantaneously make decisions.

> By superposing itself in [the brain] an infinite number of paths—*all* possible ones—*an electron is able to search simultaneously for the most efficient one.* The protein responds to the electron shifts by changing its conformation. The new conformation, in turn alters the probabilities that determine the different paths and alters as well their relative efficiencies. . . . There is, in other words, a continuous feedback process that is as close to instantaneous as one might imagine.[8]

In *The Quantum Brain,* Santinover further describes the brain as a self-organizing system which has a "tendency toward *chaos*. . . . Chaos does *not* mean disorder; the proper term is 'deterministic chaos.'"[9] Both chaos theory and the science of complexity relate to the brain. In Capra and Luisi's research:

> When the study of consciousness is approached by braiding together experience, neurobiology, and nonlinear dynamics, the "hard problem" turns into the challenge of understanding and accepting two new scientific paradigms. The first is the paradigm of complexity theory.[10]

Jeffrey Santinover elaborated on this paradigm shift: *"[The brain] learns by itself, from experience, and embeds the lessons of experience by reconfiguring its own hardware.* . . . Systems such as the brain *organize themselves* into higher and higher levels of information-processing capacity. Global intelligence . . . emerges bottom-up from purely local interaction."[11] Not only do we impact or change the environment, but it impacts and changes us at the same time.

SPACE TIME

We learned in chapter 2 that space and time are part of the same continuum; we cannot speak of one without the other. We also have now learned that, "Spacetime not only curves; it also vibrates . . . it's not only warped, it's dynamic."[12] Capra expressed how this understanding came to be:

> [P]articles must not be pictured as static three-dimensional objects, like billiard balls or grains of sand, but rather as four-dimensional entities in space-time. Their forms have to be understood dynamically, as forms in space and time. Subatomic particles are dynamic patterns which have a space aspect and a time aspect. Their space aspect makes them appear as objects with a certain mass, their time aspect as processes involving the equivalent energy.[13]

These notions of space time and four dimensionality are confounding. We think in terms of three-dimensions, so a 3D graphic depiction might be of assistance, here. Roger Penrose used an M. C. Escher print (see figure 4.1) to illustrate. In Penrose's own words:

> This is Escher's description of the Universe—you see it is full of angels and devils! A point to note is that it looks [has the perception] as though the picture get very crowded towards the edge of the limit circle. This occurs because this representation of hyperbolic space is drawn on an ordinary plane sheet of paper, in other words, in Euclidian space. What you have to imagine is that all the devils are supposed to be actually exactly the same size and shape so that, if you happened to live in this Universe towards the edge of the diagram, they would look exactly the same to you as the ones in the middle of the diagram.[14]

This shows the curved nature of space. If you were observing on the edge, the devils would look big to you. Space is *relative* to the observer. If you were to move from the center of the two-dimensional space to the edge it would not take long. However, if this were a three-dimensional space, it would take longer to get from the space spot to what appeared to be the edge in the two-dimensional space. This shows the curvature of space. The same phenomenon exists when we imagine the expansion of space time; the time is actually the fourth dimension.

Figure 4.1 Dimensionality. *Source*: 487299315.

So, not only does space warp, but so does time. Gravity, according to Einstein, *is* the warping of space and time.[15] Brian Greene went on to explicate:

> Much like a rubber membrane on which a bowling ball has been placed, the fabric of space becomes distorted due to the presence of a massive object like the sun . . . the shape of space *responds* to objects in the environment. . . . Unlike Newton, Einstein has specified the *mechanism* by which gravity is transmitted: the warping of space. In Einstein's view, the gravitational tether holding the earth in orbit is not some mysterious instantaneous action of the sun; rather, it is the warping of fabric caused by the sun's presence.[16]

Professor of physics at Brown University, Stephon Alexander, noted that *gravity* is caused by space and time bending, and that the *observer* is a critical feature in the equation. He describes the work of twins Ryan and Trevor Oakes—artists in New York City. They show how light is perceived by the observer by looking at light over a spherical (concave) surface. The way in which they paint shading makes a three-dimensional image appear from a two-dimensional canvas. Such an illustration can help us perceive how we might imagine a fourth dimension in our visual three-dimension world.

Alexander explains, "Like space and time, light also becomes a four-dimensional entity. In this view Einstein realized that electric and magnetic fields were three-dimensional projections of a four-dimensional light wave."[17] In much the same way, we all have seen the ripple effect on the surface of a pond as a stone is tossed into the pond. We see the ripples radiate outwards, but there are similar ripples that we cannot see radiating out in three-dimensional space. While we don't see this three-dimensional radiation, it is simple enough for us to comprehend. Now, we have to imagine, since we already have learned that we live in a four-dimensional world, that there is a fourth-dimensional radiation, too, that of time.

This drives home the point that perception is everything. John Gribbon noted, "Remember, that although we *perceive* a flow of time that does not necessarily mean that there *is* a flow of time."[18] In the words of Fritjof Capra, "Since space and time are now reduced to the subjective role of the elements of the language a particular observer uses for his or her description of natural phenomena, each observer will describe the phenomena in a different way."[19]

This finding has profound implications for science, and ultimately for the understanding of our human organizations. "In thermodynamic equilibrium, there is no way to distinguish the past from the future."[20] Indeed, if this is the case, then the future can predict the present. That is worth repeating and will be described in chapter 5—the future can predict the present!

THE BIG BANG, BLACK HOLES, AND PARALLEL UNIVERSES

The Big Bang theory has been in vogue and at the same time much maligned, but physicists cannot break away from it. It is accepted that the universe started at a singularity where all matter, time, and space began in one tiny bundle. It has continued to go through inflation ever since—these past 13.8 billion years.[21] However, again, as we have learned previously, this inflation has not taken place in a three-dimensional expanse, but rather in a four-dimensional expanse (the fourth dimension being time). Everything that exists today came from this original singularity.

This ab initio theory only has led to other scientific explanations, theories, and insights. Einstein struggled to accept quantum physics. However, a connection may have been made between relativity and quantum physics. Brian Greene posits on the development of string theory: "Within this new framework, general relativity and quantum mechanics *require one another* for the theory to make sense. According to superstring theory, the marriage of the laws of the large and the small is not only happy but inevitable."[22] He elaborated, "String theory appears to resolve the conflict between general relativity and quantum mechanics . . . string theory provides a truly unified theory, since all matter and all forces are proposed to arise from one basic ingredient, oscillating strings."[23]

The science of holograms emerged from quantum physics. A hologram is a combination of two waves intersecting (an interference pattern) creating a 3D image. Each portion of a holographic film contains the full hologram, but each individual slice is less clear than the original. In *The Holographic Universe*, Michael Talbot discusses the work of a protégé of Albert Einstein, David Bohm, expressing the wholeness, as opposed to separateness, of things:

> Because everything in the cosmos is made out of the seamless holographic fabric of the implicate order, he believes it is . . . meaningless to view the universe as composed of "parts." . . . Despite the apparent separateness of things at the explicate level, everything is a seamless extension of everything else, and ultimately even the implicate and explicate orders blend into each other. . . . Things can be part of an undivided whole and still possess their own unique qualities.[24]

This logic led Bohm to believe that the entire universe is a hologram, and what we see literally encompasses everything in the universe across space and time. In Talbot's words, "Just as every portion of a hologram contains the image of the whole, every portion of the universe enfolds the whole . . . the whole past and implications for the whole future are also enfolded in each small region of space and time."[25]

Bohm's vision didn't stop at the universe; he brought his thinking down to the human dimension. According to Capra, Bohm described this view as,

> "holomovement" for the ground of all manifest entities. The holomovement . . . is a dynamic phenomenon out of which all forms of the material universe flow. . . . According to Bohm, space and time, too, emerge as forms flowing out of the holomovement; they, too, are enfolded in the explicate order. . . . Bohm found it necessary to regard consciousness as an essential feature of the holomovement. . . . He sees mind and matter as being interdependent and correlated, but not causally linked.[26]

Taking this notion of holographs down further to the human brain, neuroscientist Karl Pribram extrapolated from this reasoning:

> This was precisely the feature that got [him] so excited, for it offered at last a way of understanding how memories could be distributed rather than localized

in the brain. If it was possible for every portion of a piece of holographic film to contain all the information necessary to create a whole image, then it seems equally possible for every part of the brain to contain all of the information necessary to recall a whole memory.[27]

The implications of holographic thinking could have staggering implications for our organizational structures. Every part of our organizations would encapsulate the entire structure, including past, present, and future. This notion will be explored in a more thoughtful way in the next chapter.

Before concluding, let's shift to two even more explosive, and interconnected, theories—that of the Big Bang and Black Holes. While physicists struggle with the notion of the Big Bang, they have not been able to dispel it, and the theory has become accepted as the best possible theory of how our universe began. At the point of the singularity, where even time did not exist, all matter and energy that ever existed, still exists, and will ever exist was compressed into a tiny mass of matter and energy. This mass has been expanding, albeit unevenly—like ripples on a pond, ever since.

To understand the Big Bang even better, we must explore Black Holes for a moment. Einstein's general theory of relativity pointed in the direction of Black Holes where gravity builds on itself as all matter, energy, and even light is pulled into a singular place just beyond what is known as the event horizon, most often from the collapsing of massive stars.[28] Black Holes make time slow down via Einstein's notion of "frame-dragging."[29] All this interconnectedness coming together in one place means that even space and time become irrelevant or nonexistent. Does this not create an eerie recollection of how the Big Bang started?

A universe might be created out of a blackhole from another universe. It has now been suggested that what lies on the other side of a black hole is an ever-expanding white hole[30] where a new universe may be created, via a process known as quantum looping, out of all the matter and energy from the previously existing universe. This notion is like a bouncing ball where the same universe keeps recreating itself. (See figure 4.2)].

At a universe's birth, it had zero-dimensions of time or space. Stephen Hawking and James Hartle (University of California Santa Barbara) believed that when our universe originated at the Big Bang, there was no such thing as time, so in that respect there was no beginning.[31] Hawking talked of back-to-back shuttlecock depictions of the start of the universe. At his death, Hawking was wrestling with a holographic universe model.[32]

Another suggestion of how these multiple universes occur comes from the notion of quantum tunneling. Such a tunnel does not pinch off the old universe; rather, it is like an umbilical cord connecting the two. Jeffrey Santinover expressed:

Figure 4.2 Birth of a New Universe from a Black Hole. *Source*: Francesca Vidotto.

[C]haos in a quantum aggregate directly pushes small differences upward in scale (rather than destroying them, as had been assumed) and makes them more persistent. The presence of tunneling makes quantum chaos more likely, and quantum chaos tends to enhance tunneling.[33]

Might these indeed be examples of a new Big Bang, the creation of a new universe out of the same matter and energy? Would this then be a parallel universe or maybe a "multiverse?" Would this be a hologram? Did our universe come from another universe? For the sake of creating a new vision for our organizations, it may be irrelevant whether these multiple realities are born from tunneling, bouncing balls, shuttlecocks, black and white holes, or other theories. What does matter is that our visions of our organizational worlds must be reconsidered.

One final thought that continues to be re-emphasized throughout these dynamic sciences is the notion of interconnectivity and of networking. Even multiple or parallel universes exhibit these notions. There is application of these principles to our humanness. All educators are quite familiar with Abraham Maslow's Needs Hierarchy. We learned that there are five ever higher needs all humans share: physiological; safety; belongingness and love; esteem; and, self-actualization. In its simplest form, people are motivated by their level of needs, always striving for the next level on the hierarchy but must fulfill the previous need-level before moving up to the next.

However, Maslow's later work (unknown to many of us) expanded to include: cognitive; aesthetic; and transcendence.[34] The former two are immediately after esteem and just prior to self-actualization. It is this highest level, transcendence, which is most applicable to the principles herein. People are most motivated when they are not self-actualized in isolation, but when they are transcended by values to be interconnected with nature and with others.

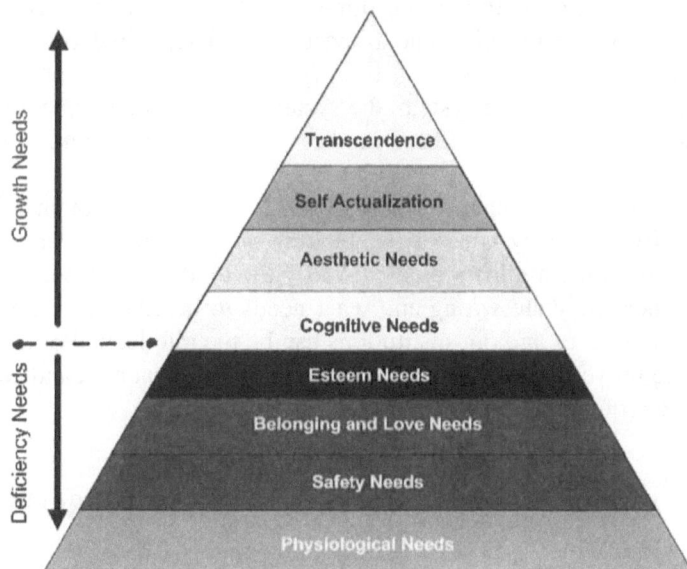

Figure 4.3 Maslow's Hierarchy of Needs. *Source*: Saul McLeod, "Maslow's Hierarchy of Needs," Simply Psychology, March 20, 2020), https//:www.simplypsychology.org/maslow.html.

This is when we get the most out of ourselves and the most out of our organizations—when we network and connect with one another. (See figure 4.3).

LESSONS LEARNED

While many lessons have been reinforced from early understandings of quantum physics, new ideas have emerged, as well. These lessons will be noted here and will be fleshed out in the final chapter.

- The entire system is a living, dynamic, thinking system.
- Like holographs, each part of the system contains the entire system—the entire system lies within each part.
- There are dual aspects—a complementarity—within the system; both process and structure.
- There is interconnectedness of all parts of the systems which experiences nonlocal causality.
- Continuous feedback loops are inherent throughout the system.
- There are multiple potentialities or possibilities at once.
- Deterministic chaos is a creative force and drives the system.

- The system self-organizes from the bottom up.
- There system exists within a four-dimensional reality of space and time.
- The observer is subjective and impacts the system, and observation is relative.
- While people impact the system, the system impacts the people, too.
- Time is not linear; the future can predict or impact the present.

Before we conclude this chapter, there is a body of research known as Critical Theory. Critical Theory is a way of looking at organizations, and the way we administrate them allows us a path to view their attributes critically, to examine where they are wrong and what needs to be changed. This way of examining ourselves and our institutions can be the intellectual bridge which allows us to move from the antiquated to the vibrant, dynamic, and adaptable systems we require.

CRITICAL THEORY IN A QUANTUM UNIVERSITY

We have learned so many lessons from these newer sciences. Critical Theory can provide the vehicle to re-examine our present understandings and assumptions of our organizations and of our leadership. Through a critical analysis we can determine what aspects we must keep and those that we must jettison and create anew. A poignant literary caricature of critical thinking drives home the point:[35]

> *People of discretion. Experts. I do not like experts. They are our jailors. I despise experts more than anyone on earth. . . . They solve nothing! They are servants of whatever system hires them. They perpetuate it. When we are tortured, we shall be tortured by experts. When we are hanged, experts will hang us. . . . When the world is destroyed, it will be destroyed not by madmen but by the sanity of its experts and the superior ignorance of its bureaucrats.*[36] ~~le Carre

These lines of a Soviet scientist in John le Carre's novel, *The Russian House,* capture the essence of workers' deepening frustrations to those individuals who have authority over them. Unbeknownst to many contemporary administrative practitioners this emotes the body of research called Critical Theory.

This research has remained on the fringe of administrative preparation programs because of its revolutionary bent and because of its lack of prescription. More succinctly, it's too radical with no perceived practical application for our leaders.

Critical Theory is just that. It's a theory (or better—a way of thinking) that is critical of the way things are. Critical theorists question everything. They question the status quo, power and authority structures, even their own motivations. They look to truly empower workers. "Critical theory exposes abuses by elites and explores alternatives, more democratic and egalitarian models of organization."[37]

Proponents of Critical Theory desire bosses and workers alike to examine the status quo, to examine our assumptions of power relationships and of decision-making protocols, and to examine what we take for granted in our institutions.[38] In order to take a critical look at these assumptions, procedures, and relationships people need to enter processes of substantive dialogue. They must be allowed to express dissenting opinions without fear of subtle reprisal—to speak truth to power.

A low-level employee needs to be secure when challenging power and authority in their institution. During the Industrial Age, management controlled with an iron fist. Everyone knew where they stood in the organization. The shift to the modern era of Human Relations Approaches has made the power dynamic more murky to see. According to Jermier:

> Contemporary mechanisms of control are often unobtrusive. . . . Although organizational theorists have long acknowledged that processes of control are integral to the way organizations operate there are reasons to believe that we have entered a new age in which the forms of control being used are more insidious and widely misunderstood.[39]

Therefore, the manipulation of Human Resources Management is unethical and tricks employees into feeling they are empowered, when in fact, they are not.[40] Faculty and staff are asked to work on committees that carry out the vision of their superiors. Yet they have no real say in the vision. They set their goals, but the goals are from an allotment approved by administration. They are mentored into the ways of the system and told, "This is the way we do things around here." They become corporate clones embraced with group-think.

Employees have worked hard to get and maintain these jobs. They are compensated fairly well and have good health and retirement benefits. In other words, they have become comfortable, with too much to lose, to speak out against the group-think. When a subordinate voices dissidence, they could lose everything. So they keep quiet and don't verbalize their objections. This inaction is repeated every day across the organization. Workers have become victims of their own success.

Critical Theory asks employees and employers to question power relationships and motives of those making the decisions. While Critical Theory not only criticizes the status quo, it also looks to truly empower employees through democratic processes. In the words of Maxim Voronov and Peter Coleman, "Critical theory seeks to expose instances in which ideology constrains and oppresses certain groups while giving unfair advantage to others and to create more democratic workplaces."[41]

Critical Theory has taught us to be wary of hierarchical structures. There is little doubt that hierarchies and their corresponding bureaucracies have taken on a life of their own—a life that is choking out the life of the creative people who populate them. Furthermore, Critical Theory demands that those in power continually reflect upon their actions and policies to evaluate both their purposes and their effects.

Critical Theory has direct application to our institutions of higher learning. The most obvious impact is on our shared governance models and decision-making. The executive administration sets direction, creates expectations, and inspects the professionals' progress toward those expectations. When they cut budgets, senior administrators make decisions with "patriarchal compassion."

This statement may seem over the top; however, it is quite likely the reader has served on committees where the group had made a decision only to be overturned by the administration. It must be noted that these committees of educators typically truly only can make recommendations—they have no real authority. This is very routine, and it has created terrible morale issues among professors.

There is an alternative, however. Democratic decision-making processes and dialogue are central features to any system that chooses to provide a critical praxis and dialectic as defined by Paulo Freire.[42] Critical dialogue is the vehicle for practitioners to become aware of their condition, their promise, and how to get there.[43]

In other words, the professional workplace must offer a time and a place for faculty and staff to have honest and open dialogue. They must feel free to express themselves, to have transparent dialogue and come to reasoned conclusions together. They must be able to speak truth to power. Critical Theory can help us move our organizations from a Closed model to an Open model and will be explored in the final chapter of this book.

ESSAY—DR. MARTIN TADLOCK

University Leadership: Preserving the Essence of Education

In 1938 John Dewey said: "What avail is it to win prescribed amounts of information about geography and history, to win ability to read and write, if in the process the individual loses his or her soul; loses appreciation of things worthwhile, of the values to which these things are relative; loses desire to apply what has been learned and, above all, loses the ability to extract meaning from future experiences as they occur."[44]

In 1955, James Mursell pointed out:

> If the schools of a democratic society do not exist for and work for the support and extension of democracy, then they are either socially useless or socially dangerous. At the best they will educate people who will go their way and earn their living indifferent to the obligations of citizenship in particular and of the democratic way of life in general. . . . But quite likely they will educate people to be enemies of democracy—people who will fall prey to demagogues, and who back movements and rally round leaders hostile to the democratic way of life. Such schools are either futile or subversive. They have no legitimate reason for existence.[45]

As I discovered long ago, the label "higher education" refers to chronology and has nothing to do with a more progressive state of knowledge or application of leadership principles as compared to K–12 education. In fact, after serving in a variety of leadership positions within higher education over the past thirty years, I believe most higher education leaders ignore democratic principles of shared governance, live unexamined lives, and are clueless about Critical Theory and its application instructionally or administratively.

While many of us ascribe to the tenets of Critical Theory as reviewed in this and the following chapter, in my experience the implementation of practices reflecting those tenets is conspicuously absent in the classrooms, board rooms and conference rooms of a campus. Even with tremendous gains in the use of technologies that help democratize society, not much has changed in how we run our colleges and universities.

We teach and meet in ways that are unexamined and undemocratic, and there seems to be no move to do otherwise. As universities become ever more selective and exclusive, fixated on rankings and national branding along with the crisis of the day, critically examining the fundamental purposes of public education and the role of colleges and universities as democratic sites continues to be an unvisited conversation among higher education leaders.

Core Beliefs

It may be helpful to understand that this essay is built upon a personal set of educational beliefs formulated in response to a capstone class assignment while enrolled in Miami University's doctoral program in educational administration from 1986 to 1990, after having taught middle schoolers for five years. That assignment forced me to call into question my own thinking about everything from personal values to societal structures of power to beliefs about the role of public education.

The resulting draft helped me design instructional and administrative practices to align with those beliefs. It gave me direction and hope as a faculty member and administrator working within the pervasive authoritarian structures so often encountered in classrooms, conference rooms and board rooms. While not original in their origin since some are shamelessly borrowed from John Dewey's educational creed, these beliefs helped me rethink my own practices.[46]

Here are those beliefs, based upon being in public education my entire career:

1. Higher education is a process of living and not a preparation for living. The university/college is the "real world" just as life outside of the university/college is the "real world." To tell students "just wait until you are in the real world" denigrates the university/college, depicting it as a place where daily life doesn't really matter and neither do the lives of those who labor here, learn here, struggle here, and celebrate here.
2. Everyone at the university is a teacher; and everything teaches. Every interaction. Some teach in formal classroom settings; but all of us teach through every interaction with a student or community member.
3. Teaching and learning is pre-eminent but integrated with a pervasive value for the discovery and application of knowledge. That is what we do as a teaching and learning organization. However, higher education should be a democratic site where we value and live democratic principles of inclusion, rational dialogue, reasoned thought, with an unrelenting commitment to social justice for all people regardless of social standing, economic capacity, race, religion, gender, ethnicity, political affiliation, sexual preference . . . categories sometimes used to marginalize those not "like us." We value those things because we are a public university of and for the people. Those values should be core to who we are and what we do.
4. The fundamental purpose of a public university/college is to integrate community life into the educational process and the educational process into the community. The label of public means that the university/college is dedicated to serving the common good and that it belongs to the public; the citizens of the state . . . all of them, not an elite few.
5. Education is comprised of psychological and sociological sides that cannot be separated from educational experience. The extent to which we address the personal and social concerns of students, faculty, and staff through the explicit and implicit (or hidden) curriculum will largely

determine the extent of learning and transformation that occurs within those students, faculty, and staff.
6. The university/college reflects the kind of society in which we wish to live and work and play, yet is also influences society. Democratic principles that underlie our preferred way of life in society must be lived within the educational institution if we expect our democratic way of life to flourish.
7. Education is a social process and the university/college is a social institution.

Educative and Mis-Educative

Those beliefs influenced every class taught and every administrative choice made after leaving Miami University to return to the middle school classroom in 1990, but it was not easy to live critically and democratically. While a set of core beliefs help, it continues to be a struggle for me and others to live those beliefs. While opportunities exist for university and college leaders to influence others and build frameworks leading to more critically examined, democratic practices in the college and university setting, I seldom see it done. Neither do many of my colleagues.

For example, a few months ago I attended a faculty lecture on campus about authoritarian leadership and principles espoused by Plato in contrast with principles espoused by Dewey and advocates of democratic leadership. Several interesting questions were raised during the presentation, with the first being: Isn't lecture in the instructional setting a synonym for university administration?

That question spurred discussion with two comments that received overwhelming support from the group: "Lecture is the selection of and delivery of information from an authority figure ... sounds like a typical campus meeting to me." "Any teaching or leadership approach used to deliver content with limited dialogue and engagement of the audience is authoritarianism and anti-democratic." The final question asked before leaving the room stuck with me: "Why are we doing these things in higher education?"

Failures of Leadership

One reason we lecture and use scripted meetings in colleges and universities may be for efficiency's sake. In my experience, university leaders prioritize efficiency and expediency above discussions about what is truly educative in the teaching/learning process. We fail to engage in a substantive dialogue about how educational practice reflects the democratic values and principles we say we want to see more of in this country.

We fail to engage in dialogue about what constitutes knowledge and democratic practice in the first place, how knowledge and practice is constructed and validated, and how the delivery of that knowledge can be educative and transformational or mis-educative and reductionist. We fail to acknowledge that educational settings are one of the few remaining common spaces where people may experience living democratic principles daily.

LESLIE'S LAMENT

Leslie and LaShonda found themselves side-by-side at another one of their girls' volleyball matches. They overlooked the gym from a glassed-in cafeteria for this away match. They shared a plate of nachos. During a break in the action, they continued their conversation from last week.

LaShonda began, "Leslie, I've been thinking about how I described to you my board. Really, I have two boards. I have more of an operational board—that's the one I told you of last week. But, I also have an advisory board; you might call it a board of advisors. In fact, that's the group I started with."

Leslie listened to her college roommate intently. "Tell me more, please."

"Well, when I was developing the idea for my new business, I had no idea how to do it. I called my former professor and advisor, Dr. Newton. He said I needed to put together a board of advisors. These were people who I trusted, who had some experience starting a business, and they knew the market."

"Do you still have them as an advisory board?" Leslie queried.

"For the most part, yes. We meet twice a year, and most of the original group remains. They're my brain trust, my creative and grounding force. I love them dearly. I update them with progress and struggles with my company, they give me feedback, and they share with me what changes they are seeing in their business worlds. I think we all help each other, honestly."

"That is so interesting, Shon. I don't know if the college has a board of advisors. Tell me the difference with your other board," Leslie said excitedly.

"That board is much more traditional. I'm strategic with them in a different sense. I need people with very particular skill sets and talents. I have, for example, an accountant, a lawyer, a banker, a CEO from mid-sized business, a retired HR director, and an administrator from the two-year community college."

Leslie asked, "What is their function?"

"They make sure you keep to your mission, Leslie," LaShonda continued. "They make sure your business is financially sound and viable; they make sure you are following your legal responsibilities and have ethical practices. They have expertise in running a business, and they help you to keep on that target. They should be asking you questions, and they do give some advice. And, boy, do I need their expertise!"

Leslie had her eyes closed during LaShonda's conversation; she was taking in every word. "That helps me tremendously. I have a much better understanding of my role on the college board. Now, I have to figure out my expertise. What do I have to bring to the board?"

"My goodness, Leslie," responded LaShonda, "You bring the expertise of being a teacher. And, you're a parent. You bring in real-life experience that can help keep people grounded."

"Fair enough, Shon, but that seems more like an advisory role—something akin to what you said for your board of advisors. I have a sneaky suspicion I'm on the Board of Trustees for my family's wealth," Leslie replied ruefully. "One thing for certain—I'm going to speak with President Leonard about our discussion." With that, the women turned back to the match. It was a highly competitive match and came down to the very end.

"What a fun nail-biter!" proclaimed Leslie. "Hey, I forgot to tell you. Chrissey has been accepted to Lakewood College. We're going back for a second visit, tomorrow. She's loved the tours of the other schools, too, but I think she is at the point where she just wants to make a decision, and I think she just wants to make sure this is the right one."

LaShonda gave a polite, almost forced, smile. "I'm so happy for you guys."

"LaShonda, what's wrong?" asked Leslie knowing something was amiss with her best friend.

"Tonyae is having second thoughts about college. Well, that's not totally true. She's thinking of taking a 'gap year,' and exploring life. Leslie, I'm terrified of this."

Leslie reminded LaShonda that she herself was a free-spirited entrepreneur. In fact, Tonyae was following her mother's lead, in a very real sense. "I think this is great. Like you, Tonyae has a courageous spirit and mind. What a wonderful time to explore. Those life experiences can only make her college learning more meaningful."

"I know. Thanks. But, what if she decides not to go to college afterwards?"

Leslie quickly replied, "Oh, she will, and she will come back with more focus and more maturity, and she will be a leader in her class. I remember my freshmen year in college. I enjoyed the learning, but I felt at times that I wasn't intellectually prepared. I remember taking Ulre's philosophy course. I was out of my league as a freshman. I sure wish I took that a couple of years later; I would have gotten so much out of it. Now tell me, does Tonyae have an idea what she wants to do in her gap year?"

"She has applied to the Peace Corps."

"Oh my gosh, Shon. That is fantastic. What real-world experiences she will get. And, I am aware that she will be able to apply some of those experiences directly to college credit!"

"I know, Leslie," LaShonda replied. "I guess I need to understand that her path doesn't need to follow my path or the path I envisioned for her. This really could be a good thing. I'm just going to miss my baby."

The last couple of conversations with LaShonda gave Leslie a lot of insights. She knew what she needed to do. She needed to have a chat with the college president and board chair. She was invigorated about what might be.

NOTES

1. Banesh Hoffman cited in Cole, *The Hole in the Universe*, 20.
2. Capra and Luisi, *The Systems View of Life*, xi.
3. Capra and Luisi, *The Systems View of Life*, 274.
4. Talbot, *The Holographic Universe*.

This is the case, because our brain communicates in brain *waves*. "Since brainwave patterns are not confined to any single neuron or group of neurons, but are a global property of the brain" (76). He went further:

This was precisely the feature that got [neuroscientist Karl] Pribram so excited, for it offered at last a way of understanding how memories could be distributed rather than localized in the brain. If it were possible for every portion of a piece of holographic film to contain all the information necessary to create a whole image, then it seemed equally possible for every part of the brain to contain all the information necessary to recall a whole memory (17).

5. Lipton, *The Biology of Belief*, 101–102.
6. Capra and Luisi, *The Systems View of Life*, 259.
7. Penrose, *The Large, the Small*, 133.

Echoing these sentiments, Professor Csikzentmihalyi noted, "Emotions, intentions, and thoughts do not pass through consciousness as separate strands of experience, but that they are constantly interconnected, and modify each other as they go along."

Csikzentmihalyi, *Finding Flow*, 26.

8. Satinover, *The Quantum Brain*, 184.
9. Satinover. *The Quantum Brain*, 113.
10. Capra and Luisi, *The Systems View of Life*, 261.
11. Satinover, *The Quantum Brain*, 9, 10.
12. Cole, *The Hole in the Universe*, 109.
13. Capra, *The Tao of Physics*, 203.
14. Penrose, *The Large, the Small*, 29–30.
15. Greene, *The Elegant Universe*, 67.
16. Greene, *The Elegant Universe*, 68–70.
17. Stephon Alexander, "What This Drawing Taught Me about Four-Dimensional Spacetime" *Nautilus,* (March 16, 2017).

This is a very worthwhile read as it shows pictures and diagrams explaining the narrative provided, herein. Alexander further shows the fourth dimension of "light cones" (in chart form) depicting past, present, and future time.

18. John Gribbon, *In Search of the Multiverse: Parallel Worlds, Hidden Dimensions, and the Ultimate Quest for the Frontiers of Reality* (Hoboken, NJ: Wiley & Sons, 2009), 90.
19. Capra, *The Tao of Physics*, 167.
20. Gribbon, *In Search of the Multiverse*, 97.
21. Elizabeth Howell, "What is the Big Bang Theory?" *Space.com.* (November 7, 2017). www.space.com/25126-big-bang-theory.html.
22. Brian Greene, *The Elegant Universe: Superstrings, Hidden Dimensions, and the Quest for the Ultimate Theory* (New York: Vintage Books, 2000), 4.
23. Brian Greene, *The Elegant Universe: Superstrings, Hidden Dimensions, and the Quest for the Ultimate Theory* (New York: Vintage Books, 2000), 136.

Greene went further: "String theory alters the picture [particles as matter/stuff] radically by declaring that the 'stuff' of all matter and all forces are the *same*. Each elementary particle is composed of a single string [more like a rubber band or violin string]—that is, each particle *is* a single string—and all strings are absolutely identical. Differences between the particles arise because their respective strings undergo different resonant vibration patterns" (146). [There is actually an evolution of string theory called M-Theory. (M stands for Membrane)].

24. Michael Talbot, *The Holographic Universe: The Revolutionary Theory of Reality* (New York: Harper Collins, 2011), 48.

Talbot goes on: "To illustrate what he means he points to the little eddies and whirlpools that often form in a river. At a glance such eddies appear to be separate things and possess many individual characteristics. . . . But careful scrutiny reveals that it is impossible to determine where any given whirlpool ends and the river begins" (48–49).

25. Michael Talbot, *The Holographic Universe: The Revolutionary Theory of Reality* (New York: Harper Collins, 2011), 50.
26. Capra, *The Tao of Physics*, 320.
27. Talbot, *The Holographic Universe*, 17.
28. Ethan Siegel, "Ask Ethan: Does a Time-Stopping Paradox Prevent Black Holes from Growing?" *Science,* (January 11, 2020).
29. Michelle Starr, "A Strange Black Hole is Shooting Out Wobbly Jets Because It's Dragging Spacetime," *Space,* (January 1, 2020).

At least time slows down to an outside observer. Ethan Siegel, "Ask Ethan: Does a Time-Stopping Paradox Prevent Black Holes from Growing?" *Science,* (January 11, 2020).

30. Carlo Rovelli, "Black Hole Evolution Traced Out with Loop Quantum Gravity," *Physics* (11) 127, American Physical Society, (December 10, 2018).
31. Dennis Overbye, "Infinite Visions Were Hiding in the First Black Hole Image's Rings," *The New York Times,* (March 28, 2020).

Overybye explains that the recent discoveries of the Event Horizon Telescope indicate that scientists can now see the entire universe (over space and time) in one place—the galaxy M87 in the Virgo constellation.

32. Natalie Wolchover, "Physicists Debate Hawking's Idea that the Universe had No Beginning," *Quanta Magazine,* (June 6, 2019).

33. Satinover, *The Quantum Brain*, 209.

34. Abraham Maslow, *Relgions, Values, and Peak Experiences* (New York: Penguin, 1970).

This work was cited and thoroughly explained in:

Saul McLeod, "Maslow's Hierarchy of Needs," *Simply Psychology*, March 20, 2020), https//:www.simplypsychology.org/maslow.html.

35. Rettig, *Shared Governance*.

For this section on Critical Theory, I have borrowed extensively from my recent book as noted.

36. Le Carre in Howard Zinn. This quote was cited in Howard Zinn, *Declarations of Independence: Cross-Examining American Ideology* (New York: Harper Collins, 1990).

Zinn referenced J. le Carre's *The Russian House* (Knopf, 1989), 6. Page 207. Zinn went on to express the radical nature of Critical Theory. In his words, "If those in charge of our society—politicians, corporate executives, and owners of press and television—can dominate our ideas, they will be secure in their power. They will not need soldiers patrolling the streets. We will control ourselves" 2.

37. Russ Marion, *Leadership in Education: Organizational Theory for the Practitioner* (Upper Saddle River, NJ: Merrill Prentice Hall, 2002).

38. L. Beyer, "The Value of Critical Perspectives in Teacher Education," *Journal of Teacher Education*, 52(2), (March/April 2001).

39. J. Jermier, "Critical Perspectives on Organizational Control," *Administrative Science Quarterly* 43, (1998), 235.

40. Maxim Voronov, and Peter T. Coleman, "Beyond the Ivory Towers: Organizational Power Practices and a 'Practical' Critical Post-modernism," *The Journal of Applied Behavioral Science* 39(2), (June 2003): 172.

For example, critical theorists have asserted that the quality of life, worker satisfaction, and participative management concerns expressed by human relations scholars are little more than clever ways to quell any potential for employee resistance and to increase managerial control over organizations. They argue, for example, that feeling empowered is not the same thing as being empowered. Choosing one of the limited options for getting the work done, in which both the agenda and the methods are defined by the management, is not empowering. Whereas more traditional management scholars take the managerial point of view, critical theorists take the employee perspective. The goal of critical theorists is to expose systems of domination and to reform organizations to create new organizational arrangements, which would be free of exploitive power arrangements and distorted communication. Voronov and Coleman continue, "Those in the lower echelons of the hierarchy often are 'duped' by those at the top into believing that they are empowered, although in reality they are still being controlled from above and by each other through ideology or disciplinary power" (176).

41. Voronov and Coleman, "Beyond the Ivory Towers," 173.

42. Paulo Freire, *Pedagogy of the Oppressed* (New York: Continuum, 1970).

For a most insightful examination of Critical Theory's application to the educational enterprise, the reader is encouraged to read Freire.

43. D. Comstock, "A Method for Critical Research," In *Knowledge and Values in Social and Educational Research*, eds. E. Bredo and W. Feinberg (Philadelphia: Temple University Press,1982), 382.

44. John Dewey, In *The Later Works of John Dewey, 1925–1953*, eds. Jo Ann Boydston. (Carbondale: Southern Illinois University Press, 1938a), 19.

45. James Mursell, *Principles of Democratic Education.* (New York: Norton, 1955), 3.

46. John Dewey, *Experience and Education* (New York: Kappa Delta Pi, 1938b).

Chapter 5

The Quantum University—Thought Experiment

"[This] creative process is much like Shiva's dance in Indian mythology. Shivan, Nataraja, the king of the dancers, dances under a halo of cosmic flame. In one hand, he holds fire to destroy the known world, to bring chaos and to destructure the old order; in the other hand, he holds a drum with which to welcome the new creation, the new order. In this integrated description of creation dynamics, the crucial features of the underlying mechanism are chaotic destructuring, unconscious proliferation of coherent superpositions, quantum leaps of insight, and chaotic restructuring."

—Goswami[1]

Just who in this world has learned any lessons from quantum physics and the other new sciences to apply to their organizations? The answer is simple—terrorists![2] In the second edition of Margaret Wheatley's *Leadership and the New Science*, she has written a new chapter describing how terrorists, perhaps unwittingly, have adopted techniques and strategies borrowed from the new sciences to create fluid, nimble, and adaptable networks. It is worth reading directly Wheatley's thoughts:

What are the criteria we use to judge effective leaders? They include the abilities to communicate a powerful vision, to motivate people to work hard for them, to achieve results, exceed plans, and implement change. We want their leadership to result in a resilient organization able to survive disruptions and crises, one that grows in capacity, that doesn't lose its way even after the leader retires. If we apply these criteria to the leaders of terrorist networks, they come out with high marks. It's difficult to acknowledge . . . but we have much to learn from them about innovation, motivation, resiliency, and the working of networks. New science explains the behavior of networks in great detail, because this is the only form of organization used by the planet.

> At present, we are dangerously blind to their strength because we use the wrong lens to evaluate their capacity. We use factors that apply to our world but not to theirs; to the behavior of hierarchical organizations, not to networks. . . . U.S. military commanders frequently acknowledge they are fighting a new kind of enemy. They describe this enemy as one who learns, changes, and adapts.[3]

On the other hand, our Western approach to leadership and organizational structure is no longer doing us any favors. All we need to do is look at our government's pathetic and dangerously lethargic response to natural disasters like the COVID-19 pandemic, as well as to Hurricane Katrina, and to Hurricane Dorian and subsequent earthquakes in Puerto Rico. "We don't have the organizational structures or the leadership that can respond quickly and well to these emergencies. . . . Following any disaster, we see the best of human nature and the worst of bureaucracy."[4]

In these and other similar cases, the large federal bureaucracies showed their limitations; it was the local municipalities and ad hoc group of citizens who made the difference. Our bureaucracies simply are not built to be nimble and adaptable. They are built for stable times, for continuity, and control. We hire bureaucrats to manage and to maintain equilibrium. Leaders are hired to make change. We purposefully build structures for stability. We need to build processes for adaptability—the structure-process duality and complementarity.

A significant contributor to our misguided approaches is the limit of our language and the orthodoxy of our experiences. We run our organizations like those we have experienced—our mimetic isomorphism. It was Albert Einstein who noted, "We may conclude that the mental development of the individual and his way of forming concepts depend to a high degree upon language."[5] It is interesting; we are using our language and understandings of a three-dimensional world to describe the reality of a four-dimensional world.[6]

Shimon Malin puts it another way:

> *Our language is steeped in the current paradigm.* This is a difficulty we face again and again. It is not only a difficulty of expression, it is a difficulty of thought as well. Language and thought are bound together, and both pull us toward the current paradigm by forces that are as strong as they are unconscious.[7]

Language and thought are entwined in our logic. Fritjof Capra warned, however, "Quantum theory and relativity theory, the two bases of modern physics, have made it clear that this reality transcends classical logic and that we cannot talk about it in ordinary language."[8]

Not only is our language misleading, but our experiences may not be wholly accurate. In fact, perhaps our language clouds our perceived experiences. K. C. Cole gave us an example: "Take a beam of white light—containing no color. Pass it through a prism, Presto, color. All you've done is separate the colors that were already there."[9] Rainbows are not what we perceive. Sometimes we put on sunglasses and see colors more vividly—the colors were already there, but we could not see as well. Animals can make sounds and hear sounds that we cannot. But, simply because we don't experience them, does not mean they do not exist.

Reality, truth, might actually exist other than we experience—the uncertainty principle. Our perceptions, our experiences, might not adequately reflect reality. What we need is perhaps a new language to shape our experiences and our way of thinking of leadership and our organizations.

MACRO-LESSONS LEARNED

Before we move to describing a Quantum University, let us make a quick review of lessons learned from all these newer sciences covered in the previous chapters. These lessons can be broken down into four broad categories: Interconnectedness of the Whole System; Role of the Observer; Time and Space; and, Role of Chaos and Complexity.

Interconnectedness of the Whole System

- The system is a living and dynamic network; it is natural and not a machine.
- There is a duality in nature and in all systems.
- This duality is complementary—either sides or views complete the whole.
- There is significant uncertainty with this complementarity. The Observer can never understand both dual aspects at the same time.
- There is communication at a distance across the system that can defy logic. This communication can be nonlocal and have hidden impact across the system.
- There is a holographic presence of the entire system embedded in every part of the system.

The Role of the Observer

- The observer impacts reality and the system impacts the observer.
- Observation is relative to the observer.

- Perceptions of the observer are pivotal.
- The observer can never fully understand the entire system at any moment given the uncertainty of nature's duality.

Time and Space

- Systems have a four-dimensional reality (space and time). In other words, reality must be viewed across the entire system and over time.
- Time is not linear; it is curved.
- Therefore, the future, present, and past are not linear and are not deterministic.
- The future can predict the present.
- Time and space are relative to one another and to the observer.
- Cause and effect are not only linear or wholly deterministic.
- The future is filled with probabilities, with potentials.

The Role of Chaos and Complexity

- Control and equilibrium can kill a system or organization.
- Disequilibrium and chaos are creative and make adaptive change.
- There is an underlying order to chaos—deterministic chaos. In this way chaos drives the system through self-organization.
- Change can be slow and deliberative, or it can be abrupt and disruptive.
- Small perturbations in one part of the system can make huge impact across the system.

These lessons can provide direction and insight into how we structure and operationalize our organizations, and even how we work with the people within our institutions. These applications are listed below and will then serve as the basis for describing a possible quantum university.

MAJOR APPLICATIONS

- The system or organization must be viewed as a whole and must be organic, nimble, and flexible.
- Over space (the entire organization) and over time (cycles & long-term)
- Relationships and interconnectedness are central to a healthy system.
- Communication is the lifeblood of a system and needs feedback loops.
- There is a duality and complementarity of process and structure in nature.
- Nature utilizes a system of checks and balances to maintain its health.
- Chaos and disequilibrium are critical features to a natural system. This is how systems make change in order to adapt and to create.
- Intuition is important.

We have learnt that "[t]he universe is *one invisible, dynamic whole* in which energy and matter are so deeply entangled it is impossible to consider them as independent elements."[10] To those words, Lipton adds: "almost all of the cells that make up your body are ... individual organisms that have evolved a cooperative strategy for their mutual survival ... as a nation reflects the traits of its citizens, our human-ness must reflect the basic nature of our cellular communities."[11]

"The major problems of our time are systemic problems—all interconnected and interdependent—and that, accordingly, they require systemic solutions."[12] Systemic approaches to addressing issues of interconnected communities require an "openness to adaptation."[13] St. John explains such adaptable behavior needs to be built into strategic planning efforts. "Recently, strategic theories of organization have been adapted to encourage flexibility. ... The early literature on strategic planning emphasized planning, while the newer literature emphasizes adaptive, decentralized action."[14]

This decentralization and adaptability put a greater onus at the bottom of the organizational pyramid and places more autonomy in the hands of the individual workers. We can draw an organizational parallel to the explanation provided by Francis Fukuyama on scientific freedom: "Scientific inquiry proceeds best in an atmosphere of freedom, where people are permitted to think and communicate freely, and more importantly where they are rewarded for innovation."[15] Ad hoc groups need to be able to come together to problem-solve and to disband as quickly as they are formed. They must be able to come together from across the system.

Our leaders need to provide a place for our workers to create and to think.[16] Not only do they need this space as individuals, but we need to provide this space collectively. "Creative discursive space for the discussion of critical social issues is necessary."[17] Mihaly Csikszentmihalyi elaborated on this point:

> This "public" space is where one's actions are evaluated by others, where once competes for resources, and where one might establish collaborative relationships with others. It has been argued that this public sphere of action is the most important for developing one's potential, the one where the highest risk are run by the greatest growth occurs.[18]

Margaret Wheatley provides provocative thoughts in summation; she talks for the necessity for creativity, but such creativity often flows from requisite chaos, and that collaboration is critical to this creativity—often in an ad hoc fashion. "We must engage with one another differently, as explorers and discoverers. ... We can realize that we must inquire together to find the new. We can turn to one another as our best hope for inventing and discovering the worlds we are seeking."[19]

BUILDING A CULTURE FOR A
QUANTUM UNIVERSITY

This is a time for us to create; we must break away from the bonds—the paradigms—that have tied us to our mimetic isomorphism. We need to provide for: bottom-up participation; ad hoc and dynamic empowerment; and, open communication with feedback loops. We need to embrace democratic values, principles, and processes. We must be willing to cede some control and to explore with deliberate chaos. Shimon Malin, author of *Nature Loves to Hide,* explains:

> A paradigm is nothing more than an abstraction adopted by a society at a given period in its history. Every abstraction has a restricted domain of validity. Unfortunately, members of the society implicitly accept the abstraction as absolute truth. One is conditioned by one's culture to explain away or just ignore experiences that indicate the existence of domains where the paradigm is invalid. Once in a while, however, this conditioning breaks down, and one has *a new experience*—an experience that does not fit the paradigm. Such experiences can be invaluable as indications of the limitations of the paradigm.[20]

Numerous authors, such as Cole, Santinover, and St. John, have directly connected quantum theories or modern organizational thinking to Eastern thinking such as Zen Buddhism.[21] None, however, have made such a dramatic and persuasive connection as Fritjof Capra in his *The Tao of Physics.*[22] For example, "The Eastern mystics see the universe as an inseparable web whose interconnections are dynamic and not static. . . . Modern physics, too, has come to conceive the universe as such a web of relations and, like Eastern mysticism, has recognized that this web is intrinsically dynamic."[23]

Capra goes to great lengths making these connections between Eastern philosophy and modern physics: duality of nature and complementarity, dynamic nature, interconnectivity, inseparability of the observer, limitations of language, limitations of our senses, space and time mutuality, and the holographic essence of nature where every portion contains the whole.

In the previous chapter, we discussed Critical Theory and how it can help us examine our organizational processes and leadership. Now, we can examine how it can help us make the necessary move toward a more congruent system. Critical Theory thinking makes us question everything about our organizational structures and governance; but, these structures remain steadfast, today. We have made attempts to move from Closed Systems to Open Systems thinking, but it has been difficult to make the requisite changes. In a particularly poignant fashion, Fritjof Capra observed,

[s]ocial thought in the late nineteenth and early twentieth centuries was greatly influenced by positivism, a doctrine formulated by the social philosopher August Comte. Its assertions include the insistence that the social sciences should search for general laws of human behavior. . . . It is evident that the positivist framework is patterned after classical physics. Indeed, Auguste Comte, who introduced the term, "sociology," first called the scientific study "social physics." The major schools of thought in the early-twentieth-century sociology can be seen as attempts at emancipation from the positivist straitjacket.[24]

Whereas Closed Systems approaches were deterministic and used a machine metaphor, citizens in the country felt alienated by their own organizations. It was a time of questioning those in authority—vocally and sometimes physically. It was the era of the Vietnam War, Watergate, Civil Rights, and the sentiment was, "don't trust anyone over 30!"

This new postmodern view of organizations as natural systems is antipositivistic, nondeterministic, and operates with an ecological or jungle-like metaphor. It moved from the Newtonian to the Quantum. It doesn't subscribe to the notion that there is a linear way to understand problems and a purely rational/quantitative way to administrate.

Rather, this movement born out of the 1960s believes that there is multiple and complex causation to most problems, that most decisions are not made with complete knowledge of all variables, and that organizations and their leaders are dramatically influenced by their institutions through a holistic lens and consider these systems as alive.

Like previous models, Open Systems theories arose in reaction to the shortcomings of its predecessors. "While alluring in their simplicity, mechanical concepts of school change run counter to the experience of most educators, who have learned to view all activity in schools as deeply human, subject to the baffling complexity that permeates most human endeavors."[25]

Open Systems hold that few simple cause-effect relationships exist within real-life systems. Effects are often far removed—in time and space—from their multiple causes. Further, top-down hierarchies, even though designed for efficiency, are ineffective and inefficient.

Human organizations should be considered dynamic living systems, unlike the rigid mechanical Closed Systems models that fail to interact with their environments. Whereas Closed Systems thinking took its cues from Newtonian physics, Open Systems thinking learned its lessons from the newer sciences, like quantum physics, ecology, biology, and chaos theory.[26]

Historian Jon Meacham quoted President Woodrow Wilson who stated that while America's democratic system appeared linear and clean, reality was different:

> The trouble with the theory is that government is not a machine, but a living thing . . . It falls, not under the theory of the universe, but under the theory of organic life. It is accountable to Darwin, not to Newton. It is modified by its environment, necessitated by its tasks, shaped to its functions by the sheer pressure of life. . . . Government is not a body of blind forces; it is a body of men. . . . with a common task and purpose.[27]

Numerous scholars have shown us how we can apply these lessons to our organizations.[28] The new sciences tell us that in natural systems apparent chaos and disorder might actually be a new order unfolding. The very act of control and demand for homeostasis might actually harm or even kill the organization, and certainly choke out innovation and growth.

At times we might need to allow the chaos to arise and the new order to unfold. But we must take a system-wide view.[29] Thus, we must avoid the compulsion to control and make quick decisions at times. Sometimes it is necessary to live with the uneasiness and allow the process to unfold.

Francis Newmann further explained not only that nonlinear models are most appropriate for governmental bodies, but that chaos should actually be used as a tool for dynamic growth. In his description of L. D. Kiel's work, Neumann posited,

> Kiel wrote that public administration traditionally has focused on incremental or equilibrium models, which do not account for instances when dramatic wholesale change can occur. He suggested that nonequilibrium processes appear to be more descriptive of the interactions of democratic societies, in which the political process brings external energy into the system and drives it far from equilibrium. It is the nonlinear process that allows the system to incorporate change within itself and to adapt to changing external environments. Kiel also suggested that agents can purposefully force change in organizations by energetically driving those organizations toward the points of chaotic thresholds. For example, he cited the situation in which Japanese executives intentionally drive their organizations to chaotic symmetry breaks. "Organizational upheaval is seen as positive. It creates instability, chaos, and potential for genuine qualitative change."[30]

The notion that our systems can be controlled and maintained at a state of equilibrium is erroneous. The tighter we try to squeeze our fist of control, the more the actual control or power oozes out between our fingers. We operate our organizations as if they were tightly controlled systems, but again, that control is elusive. Human organizations operate more like loosely coupled systems. "Today's large organizations are disaggregating into loosely connected clusters of autonomous business units."[31]

Rhodes explained the false sense of power within the reality of loosely coupled systems. "Note that power and control in each world [the world of planners and doers] is relatively meaningless since, in actuality, each remains relatively powerless to affect the system's results as long as they remain disconnected from each other."[32]

Proponents of the notion of loosely coupled systems believe that organizations are not nearly as tightly organized and managed in practice as one would believe by looking at work-flow charts and organizational charts. Therefore, we need to create organizational models that embrace broader involvement and participation, rather than try to control it. Every individual in the organization has the potential to make a large impact across the system.

Further, being loosely coupled is an extremely important feature in professional organizations—like universities. Professionals often operate through their intuitions and experiences; they need to be allowed to have professional autonomy. Loosely coupled systems allow for flexibility and professional autonomy.

For boards of trustees and college presidents and senior administrators, the lessons from loosely coupled systems theory are important. We must fight the compulsion to control every aspect of the institution. The power we have *over* people is a misnomer. The power we have *with* people is more the reality. We may have *formal authority* over people, but our *power* comes *with* people. We must encourage and support professional autonomy with the smallest local units of our organizations and do all we can to build connections among these loosely coupled units and provide them with all information available.

Still, boards often feel they have little control, yet they have a vested interest in maintaining the status quo. As our institutions became larger, more complex, and greater expectations put upon them, the administration felt they were losing control. Our leaders created a model for control and do everything to keep in control through their top-down bureaucratic hierarchies. Our leaders must fight this tendency. We must, in other words, not manage, but lead.

As we have learned bureaucratic hierarchies clearly have their critical limitations. These issues range from being unable to deliver the pragmatism for which they were designed to serving as dehumanizing places to work. Our current institutional structures are ineffective and inefficacious. Well-renowned political analyst for CNN and the *Washington Post*, Fareed Zakaria reported, "Historically, unchecked centralization has been the enemy of liberal democracy."[33]

So, the siloed, top-down, classical model of Closed Systems organizations is antiquated and ineffectual. But, a more professional, realistic, and natural

Open Systems model is revealed, again. It is a living, dynamic, interconnected democratic organization. Let us now create a Thought Experiment for the Quantum University.

THE QUANTUM UNIVERSITY—A THOUGHT EXPERIMENT

The quantum university will have a new metaphor, one that is an organic, dynamic, interconnected network, and takes full advantage of its humanness. Process will be paramount to its adaptability and its nimbleness, indeed to its survival. It will be a learning organization that is innovative, and communication lines are open and continually evolving. Groups will form and reform in an ad hoc nature in an amorphous manner.

From an outside observer, the system may appear to be chaotic, but there will always be an underlying order. There will be a spirit of experimentation to seek potentials and to look at any problem or issue from multiple viewpoints over space and time. Language will change from a three-dimensional stricture to a more real four-dimensional complex systems understanding. Theory X views of employees will be jettisoned for the trusting and embracing Theory Y belief.

The top-down pyramid bureaucratic model will not be replaced; it's too endemic to our ethos. But, it will be greatly enhanced with a certitude for process—the process of a faithful adherence to democratic principles, values, decision-making and operating—to principles of shared governance (see figure 3.4: Higher Education Organizational Pyramid Model with Checks & Balances on page __).

This book isn't about democratic organizations, per se, but democratic principles, values, and processes do embody a more ecological or natural model for our organizations and leadership. It is worth spending a few moments delineating these democratic attributes.[34] There are five core democratic values and four constitutional principles which fit this discussion.

Democratic Values

- Liberty: personal freedom, free flow of information and ideas, open debate, and freedom of assembly;[35]
- Common good: greater benefit for all, majority rule while protecting the rights of the minority;[36]
- Justice: fair treatment; shared decision-making;[37]
- Equality: no class hierarchy;[38]
- Diversity: diversity and representation of both the people and of opinions; and[39]
- Honesty, Openness, and Fairness: in all interactions with each other.[40]

Democratic Principles

- The rule of law,
- Checks and balances,
- Separation of powers, and
- Representative government.

The four constitutional principles are conceptually met through the three governance pillars: board of trustees, president, and faculty senate. The principle *of the rule of law* is primarily established through the codification of policies and bylaws; nobody is held to standards outside expectations as formally established.

The principles of *checks and balances* and *separation of power* are most notably met through delineated responsibilities associated with the respective pillars—described later. The principle of *representative government* is met through the faculty senate, and possibly staff councils, and student government associations.

To be clear, representational democracy should not infer that every person or group votes on every topic. In the words of Olson, "'Shared' means that everyone has a role. . . . 'Shared' doesn't mean that every constituency gets to participate at every stage. Nor does it mean that any constituency exercises complete control over the process. . . . The various stakeholders participate in well-defined parts of the process."[41] This example would closely mirror a Weberian organization as a delicate balance between professional and bureaucratic (described in chapter 1 and depicted in figure 1.1).

All institutions of higher education have three governance pillars with corresponding responsibilities: Board of Trustees, Executive, and Faculty.

Board of Trustees

- Fiduciary oversight;
- Ensure principles of shared governance are followed;
- Hiring, evaluating, and supporting the president;
- Ensure the institution is beholden to its mission;
- Strategic planning;
- Ensure all institutional policies are current and implemented;
- Protect academic freedom and institutional autonomy; and
- Operate with ethical standards.

Executive (President)

- Provide institutional leadership,
- Create and sustain institutional vision,

- Ensure academic quality and autonomy,
- Lead strategic planning,
- Oversee day-to-day operations,
- Communicate with various internal and external constituencies,
- Fundraising and advancement, and
- Operate with ethical standards.

Faculty Senate

- Ensure academic quality,
- Curriculum and instruction development oversight,
- Sets and oversee admissions standards,
- Research,
- Oversight of faculty status, and
- Operate with ethical standards.[42]

The board of trustees, the president (and administration), and the faculty each hold specific roles and responsibilities in the shared governance of their institutions. The best-run universities have governance systems that provide a great deal of respect and autonomy for one another, enjoy high degrees of transparency and information sharing, and most often find overlap in their work and communication with one another. Again, it's a delicate balance between the formal structure and the natural dynamic of professional systems and networks. There needs to be, on the other hand, a greater emphasis on shared governance processes and less on bureaucratic strictures.

There are, however, other groups who are critical to a new natural model of organizational structure and leadership, but who have often been left out of these democratic processes. These groups include students, professional staff, and external advisory groups. Each of these groups needs to be leveraged and involved to a much higher degree, following the democratic values and principles enumerated earlier.

The American Association of University Professors (AAUP), the American Council on Education (ACE), and the Association of Governing Boards (AGB) provide numerous detailed examples of how shared governance should work with explicit roles and responsibilities explicated.[43] At times, a model of shared governance is eschewed for a more inclusive model of *joint effort* which describes roles of each group beyond the three primary pillars.[44] These notions along with guidance on methods and processes to implement such a dynamic and natural model are extensively described in Rettig's earlier book, *Shared Governance: A More Meaningful Approach in Higher Education*.[45]

It is with this notion of joint effort that other groups can be better brought collectively into the system. Patrick Dolan,[46] writing about K–12 school systems, depicts perfectly a model which could parallel a nimble structure of involvement for such groups as a Board of Advisers, a Staff Council, and a Student Government Association. (See figure 5.1, below).

At the top of the pyramid is an arc depicting the three governance pillars. In higher education, those would represent the Board of Trustees, the President, and the Faculty Senate. The top third of the pyramid represents senior administration. The middle portion of the pyramid contains the units reporting to the senior cabinet (e.g., each academic college, business services, student services, advancement). In fact, each of these broad areas is represented by its own pyramid model. For example, each college would have its own pyramid led at the top by a dean. At the bottom of the pyramid would fall the students.

Along the side of the pyramid sweeps another arc. This arc represents other constituent groups. In this case, those groups would include a Board of Advisers, a Staff Council, and the Student Government Association. While they may not have a formal authoritative role in the bureaucratic pyramid, they are critical to the organization. In fact, this could be depicted as an overlay on figure 4.4 in chapter 4 which depicts shared governance processes within a bureaucratic pyramid. (See figure 5.2, below).

A board of advisers would serve a distinctive purpose to the conventional role of a board of trustees. While a traditional Board of Trustees has a

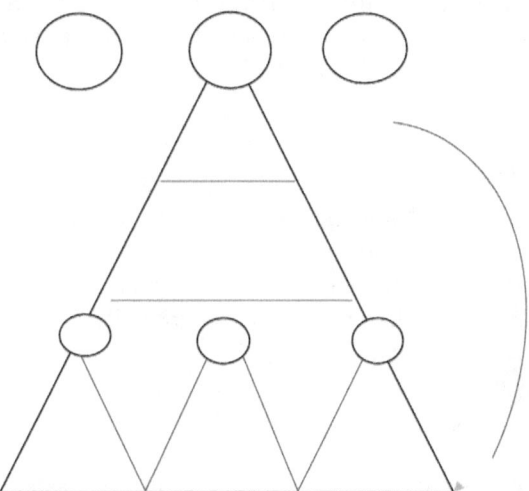

Figure 5.1 Dolan's Governance Pyramid Model. *Source*: (Adapted) Patrick Dolan. Restructuring Our Schools: A Primer on Systemic Change. Kansas City. Systems and Organizations, 1994.

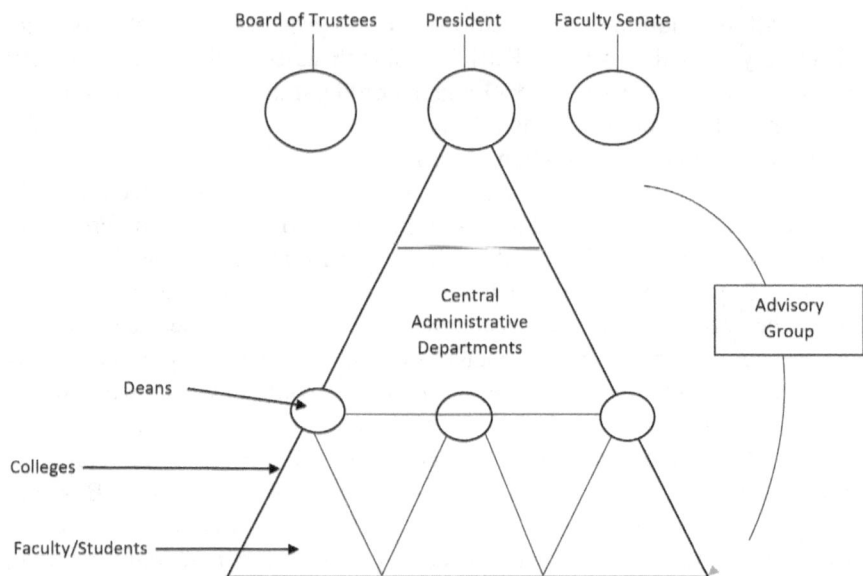

Figure 5.2 Shared Governance Involvement for Boards of Advisers, Staff Council, Student Government Association, and with a Process for Checks & Balances. *Source*: (Adapted) Patrick Dolan. Restructuring Our Schools: A Primer on Systemic Change. Kansas City. Systems and Organizations, 1994.

primarily fiduciary responsibility and makes certain the institution is beholden to its mission, has oversight of the executive, and ensures standards of ethics and policy adherence, the Board of Advisers has a unique responsibility.

Board of Advisers

- Serves as a communication and feedback loop for the community and the campus.
- It remains current with the environment, worried less about the historical mission, and more on the present and future shifts in the environment—community needs and changes.
- It focuses less on mission and more on vision with a focus toward action.
- It focuses on giving advice, thereby needing to be able to speak truth to power.
- Its membership can change in a dynamic ad hoc fashion reflecting the community.

Faculty senates are notorious for unnecessarily slowing down conversations in a spirit of academic debate. Public deliberation is a critical feature to democratic governance, but it is not healthy if it goes into a black hole—pun intended. Deliberative dialogue helps to make certain poor judgments are not made and that better solutions can be found. With that said, faculty senates (and any other deliberative body—e.g., advisory groups) need to balance deliberation with a sense of action with all due alacrity).

Such a model of inclusivity will provide for more bottom-up empowerment. With such rights of empowerment will come equal responsibility; these newly empowered groups will own their decisions. With the opportunity comes the ownership. They will look to the future and the opportunities it holds in order to create the present course of action. No longer will they be told what to do, for when someone is told what to do, the teller owns it, not the person who is told. The responsibility moves from the boss to the professional—that professional who is self-motivated, earnest, intelligent, and desires to be part of something bigger.

ESSAY CONTINUED—DR. MARTIN TADLOCK

A few years ago, I re-read *Pedagogy of the Oppressed* by Paulo Freire. He described a participatory, guided process where participants engage in dialogue about their personal and social concerns (concerns that dominate their thinking and their lives), plan how to address those concerns through social action, and then receive ongoing mentoring.

For me, Freire's work reinforces what most teachers of young adolescents learn early in their careers, that is, learning is socially constructed and it requires ongoing guidance and action to be transformative. Learning is not knowledge delivered by an authority isolated from action. Outside of the classroom, leaders who ignore those tenets when attempting to lead a college or university risk creating mis-educative, reductionist settings where democracy is an abstraction rather than a lived experience.[47]

I also re-read *Teachers as Intellectuals* by Henry Giroux, who reminds us that teachers who understand the power of engaging democratically based pedagogical practice and connecting students to substantial societal issues relevant to their lives, transforms those lives. Teachers able to engage students in active learning and intimately connect content to action are intellectuals. They are the antithesis of knowledge givers. Intellectuals do not deliver pre-packaged curricula or prescribe standardized tests and measures.

They know that transformative educational experiences and deep learning intimately connected to content doesn't occur through authoritarian approaches where pre-packaged curricula is delivered and students are assessed on how well they have absorbed that curricula. Transformative learning comes from transformative teaching and engages the mind, heart, and hands in addressing students' passion. If true for students, then would not it hold true for faculty, staff, and other members of the greater university community?[48]

Faculty, staff, and members of the university community can actively participate in leadership of the educational institution through the revamping of the myriad array of meetings, work groups, task forces, and committees that pervade the work of the bureaucracy we call higher education. Authoritarian approaches can be replaced by opportunities to engage in dialogue that results in social action to transform the institution and community into a more democratic sphere. Let's take one example.

Rosa Parks attended the Highlander School in Tennessee in 1955 to learn about school desegregation, returning to Alabama where she joined a network of people who acted to help change America. She didn't sit in a lecture hall taking notes about injustices that affected her and others every minute of every day and then take a test on the material; she engaged in a process at Highlander where dialogue, integrated with content and guidance from experienced teachers (mentors and guides), helped her create a deep understanding of the need for social action along with an awareness of how to act.

Learning was an active process at Highlander where participants engaged in conversation with others about personal and social concerns, where material relevant to those conversations was read and discussed, and where plans were drafted to act purposely involving the mind, heart, and hands. Learning was active; instruction was democratically based with expert guidance from others. Instructional time was not filled with authoritarian lectures, passive note taking, or reading material from a textbook unconnected to the concerns of participants.[49]

In sum, to be educative and transformational, educational settings should be sites that bring people together to critically examine their own beliefs through dialogue around issues that connect to personal and social concerns and prompt action where knowledge is applied under the guidance of experienced teachers or leaders.

The mind, the heart and the hands are engaged. Passive settings where an authority delivers content or instructions unconnected to personal and social concerns and without a chance for dialogue and questioning is mis-educative. Yet, we continue to legitimize such approaches in university classrooms and meeting rooms despite our acknowledgement of the need to do otherwise.

The Age of COVID

In the age of COVID, will we further validate authoritarian methods of content packaging and delivery under the label of "education" and refer to it as the next "new normal"? Will we continue to celebrate the acquisition of content to pass a test as educational? Will we continue sending a constant and powerful message to the world that education isn't about transforming lives, acting to improve conditions around us, or helping us understand how to live democratic principles that form the very foundations of a democratic society; rather is about passively gathering content, taking a test, getting a credential, and making money? Will we continue to hold virtual meetings with faculty and staff that use an authoritarian approach, talking through an administrative agenda that is directive rather than dialogical?

If so, then democratic values and democratic principles will continue to be outside of the core purposes of educational practice, and we will need to assume at least partial blame for that. As college and university leaders, we have accepted massive online learning, programmed learning, absorption of content, and screen time as valid methods of instruction. We sat in lectures, took notes, and accepted in silence what was said. We performed very well in tests and gained our credentials. We lectured. We have done to others what was done to us.

In the age of COVID, we continue to set up meetings with administrative agendas and strict timelines with little opportunity for critical examination of the institution and what we practice and why. We do not invite dialogue about critical issues confronting the future of higher education in a nation where democracy is at risk. We do not speak up publicly for fear of being fired. Therefore, we are no better than those who see education as a process of taking existing knowledge, packaging it, and selling it to the masses at the lowest possible cost in order to secure a workplace credential.

If this continues, where will we go as a country founded on democratic principles of free speech, social action, and engagement of an educated citizenry? How can a democracy sustain itself when the delivery of knowledge and the development of intellectual leaders are dominated by authoritarian approaches, now with enhanced screen time? What happens to other approaches that encourage more democratic engagement such as embedding field experience and service learning within the curriculum; inquiry-based approaches; flipped classrooms, experiential and project-based learning; analysis of real-world case studies, Socratic dialogue, and an ever-present focus on problem solving and critical thinking—all proven to be highly effective.

Those approaches are based upon a history of progressive, constructivist educational practices in Europe and the United States dating from the late 1700s and the work of Pestalozzi and others, through the 1800s with Montessori, and through the 1900s and the work of Dewey and the Progressive Education Association then into the modern era with the ongoing work of critical theorists like Freire and Giroux. You can find a similar history of experiential and progressive educational thought and practices among indigenous populations in the United States and elsewhere. Their work can lead us to transform the classroom, but can it also lead us to transform our approach to educational leadership?

Closing Thoughts

Constructivist, progressive educational models that engage students in a partnership with the teacher to build a curriculum around challenging outcomes, design experiential learning activities to meet those outcomes, and jointly assess attainment of those outcomes, work. They are not new. They exemplify what it means to be educative. Approaches based upon those models are heavily researched, reviewed, and practiced and have been written about for over 300 years.

Just as importantly, those models align with the democratic principles we should espouse and live as a public university. As faculty, how can we ask for and expect inclusion in shared decision-making and expect our voice to be heard if we then turn around and exclude students from decisions regarding the content of the curriculum, the learning activities undertaken to learn that curriculum, and the assessment practices used to determine how well they have learned?

Could those models also serve us as university leaders in building new approaches to developing future administrators and in our everyday leadership responsibilities? How can we as university leaders expect our voice to be heard among faculty, staff and community if we exclude members of those groups from engaged dialogue in university decision-making processes?

Likewise, how can we say that we value diversity when we standardize the curriculum, standardize our teaching approaches, and standardize the assessment of learning to be more efficient . . . or do the same thing when building our meeting agendas? While there are common knowledge and skill sets we could all agree upon as important for everyone, how can we address the core purposes of an institution of higher education if we fail to include student voice in decisions about their learning and fail to include faculty, staff, and community members in active decision-making about the future of the institution?

We should celebrate educational experiences that are rigorous, peer-reviewed, and research-driven; experiences that engage students in relevant, hands-on learning and critical thought; and we should build courses with students that provide those experiences. Faculty and staff can do that. They can redesign courses built around progressive, constructivist principles; include students in the design of the curriculum, learning activities, and assessment measures for those courses; build those courses as blended/hybrid courses; and collect impact data on student engagement and learning after implementation.

Administrators can build inclusive agendas and opportunity for meaningful dialogue into committee, task force, and work group meetings.

As leaders, we have an opportunity to turn the conversation about a "new normal" from one of economic devastation and the transformation of education as a predominately online arena where virtual delivery of content and virtual interactions of humans is the rule to a conversation about how universities can reinvigorate democracy through living democratic principles as they emerge from the impact of a significantly disruptive event. This may be the opportunity of a lifetime.

And in the end, why does it matter?

As stated by Thomas Jefferson in 1816, "Enlighten the people generally, and tyranny and oppressions of body and mind will vanish like evil spirits at the dawn of day . . . I believe it [human condition] susceptible of much improvement and most of all, in matters of government and religion; and that the diffusion of knowledge among the people is to be the instrument by which it is affected."[50]

You can't value democracy when you espouse the principles but live them in a way that fails to enlighten the people.

LESLIE'S LAMENT

Leslie sat at the distinguished conference room table in President Leonard's office. It was only the second time she enjoyed this privilege. The furniture was a rich cherry wood that was perfectly polished, and the executive-style papered walls held pictures of the campus from previous eras. This place felt important, Leslie thought to herself. Across the table sat the Board of Trustees chair, Edward Donaldson. Immediately to her right, at the end of the table, sat President Leonard. President Leonard and Leslie spoke on the telephone at some length last week about her ideas. He was quite interested and called for today's meeting with the board chair.

President Leonard began, "Edward, Leslie and I have a notion that we would like to run by you. I'm very intrigued by its potential. Since it's her idea, I'd like for her to begin."

"Edward, the Board of Trustees is made up of eighteen distinguished community leaders, corporate leaders for the most part. Their role is critical to the integrity of our university; but, my role doesn't seem to match the focus of this board," Leslie nervously said.

"Oh, I disagree, Leslie," came Chairman Donaldson's quick reply.

"Just a moment, please, Edward," interjected President Leonard. "Leslie has some interesting thoughts. Leslie, please continue."

"I'm not a prototypical board of trustees member. I don't have a business acumen, and I'm not a community leader. But, I do have professional insights and community connections that I think can be valuable to Southbey. In fact, I think there are plenty of other people like me who are not being utilized but could add so much to our university. We need to capitalize on these internal and external professionals and create a network across the community. Let's leverage individual strengths collectively."

As President Leonard brought forward an old-fashioned flip chart with several prepared hand-written diagrams, Leslie added: "As a quick aside, I know the board plans to increase the financial giving of each board member from $5,000 to $10,000. I can't afford it, quite frankly. And, by having this expectation of board members, you will always limit a large segment of professional community expertise from participating. Many outstanding individuals cannot afford to participate—to lead."

Chairman Donaldson squinted at that note and pursed his lips taking in a deep breath. He was a bit taken aback, but her concern made sense.

President Leonard jumped right into the charts. He showed the corporate pyramid model with the three anchors on top and restated the role of the board of trustees and of the president. He also shared the rather nascent role of the faculty senate.

Leslie then introduced the next chart showing the same pyramid model with a superimposed circle, as well as an arching line along the side to represent a Board of Advisers. She explained her goal was to create processes to help better connect silos and to bring in other voices to the campus daily operations. This would also help the campus to better connect to the outside community.

"Who would you have on this Board of Advisors, Leslie?" asked Mr. Donaldson.

"I don't have particular names, Edward," Leslie continued. "But, I know the kinds of people we're looking for. We want people representing social and civic organizations, parents, people from small businesses not represented on the Board of Trustees. We want recent graduates and a current student or two. And, just as importantly, we want professionals from the university itself. For example, I think we should have not only someone representing the faculty, but we should have various staff members representing Admissions, Financial Aid, Athletics, Student Life, Counseling, Career Services, and the Alumni Board."

Leslie could see a small smile come across Chairman Donaldson's face. Was he pleased or did he think this was silly? He finally responded, "Are we just going to create another layer of authority—more bureaucracy?"

President Leonard put up his hand. "No, Edward. This body has no formal authority. They don't make decisions, but they may make recommendations.

Their role is to dialogue and to listen to one another. Their role is to bring the community into the university, and the university into the community. They are to help create a complex network which feeds on itself. In fact, at times we might find their membership changes along with changes on campus or in the community. So, while they wouldn't have formal authority, they would have power—the power to make a difference, to help us be more adaptive, to make change."

Now the smile on Mr. Donaldson's face could not betray his interest. "Tell me more."

President Leonard continued, "I'm going to create a Staff Council. It will be made up of only professional staff from across the institution. Their job will be to better communicate across the units and departments. Again, they will discuss how to improve processes that touch aspects over the entire university. They can make some decisions on their own. I'd like three or four representatives from the Staff Council on the Advisory Council."

Leslie took her turn. "The Advisory Council would in turn hold an ex officio seat on the Board of Trustees. The Faculty Senate would have a member serve as an ex officio on the Trustees, as well." Leslie paused. "And, the Student Government Association would, too."

The smile left Chairman Donaldson's face. It wasn't a dismissive look or even skeptical; it was more serious. "So, they wouldn't be voting members?"

"That's correct," replied President Leonard.

I want you to know that I fully support Leslie's idea. In fact, she had a skeleton of an idea, and together we framed it out like this. With that said, I would like for Leslie to serve as the inaugural chair of the Board of Advisors and maintain her seat on the Board of Trustees. At the same time, I will work on creating a Staff Council with their charge to make better connections across the system and to deliberately analyze ways to improve cross-functional processes. Not only that, but I am going to have each of our academic deans create their own versions of Advisory Councils; councils that would be more ad hoc and dynamic, in nature. We need to do a much better job of connecting, communicating, and networking. We need to build synergies.

The meeting ended with a good sense of excitement. They agreed to have Leslie and President Leonard further develop this idea and present to the full Board of Trustees at the spring meeting. The expectation was to implement this new framework during the coming summer.

Leslie noted, "None of us knows everything, but together we can't be beat."

To which President Leonard added, "Just imagine all the possibilities—the future potential of Southbey University."

Chairman Donaldson concluded, "Let's start a little chaos, and get our creative juices going!"

Leslie thought to herself, "Who knew she could make so much change, have so much influence on the university—all by herself?"

That evening Leslie was so excited. She had a sense of purpose. She sat down at the dinner table with Chrissey, LaShonda, and Tonyae. The four of them worked together preparing their favorite comfort-food dinner, lasagna. They loved putting the layers on top of one another and bringing all the flavors together. And, the leftovers tasted even better the next day.

Tonyae announced her Peace Corps assignment to Myanmar. Chrissey announced her decision to attend Lakewood College and her major—Environmental Technology. The two girls were so excited and kept cutting each other off with their own dreams and aspirations. Laughter was ubiquitous. The mothers smiled, added a few comments here and there, smiled, and even had tears at times. Those at times were tears of fear of the unknown, and other times of joy for their young women.

This was going to be an important year for all.

CODA

How do you reform a leviathan?[51]

You have already started. You reform from within. The Quantum University exists already in a potential reality. It exists today in the minds of a small number of emerging leaders—the future is the present. We need these leaders to be courageous, to start dialogue with one another, to expand their networks. Maybe, just maybe they will see their organization collapsing in on itself—into a metaphorical blackhole, needing to emerge out the other side as a Big Bang induced new organization.

The leader's role of that quantum university becomes one of connector, enabler, empowerer, and chief storyteller. The leader will be a purposeful listener and creator of other leaders. The new leader makes certain everyone is beholden to the mission and the vision. They seek adaptability across the system, they create using deliberative chaos. They embrace the notions of Critical Theory and provide for a clear system of checks and balances.

This new leadership will embrace the values and principles of democratic decision-making and make certain the institution is beholden to them. These leaders, whether they are trustees or presidents, will ensure collaboration from within the system and look to the environment for better connections. Tomorrow's leader will be asked to do more work than ever before. Their approach will be less mechanical and more natural and dynamic. They will manage less; but indeed, they will lead.

NOTES

1. A. Goswami, "Creativity and the Quantum: A Unified Theory of Creativity," *Creativity Research Journal* 9 (1), (1996), 59.

2. Wheatley, *Leadership and the New Science*.

This section borrows extensively from Wheatley's analysis of terrorist organizations in relation to how they are organized and behave following principles of natural systems.

3. Wheatley, *Leadership and the New Science*, 179–180.

Wheatley goes on to elaborate: "Although these groups appear to be leaderless, they in fact are well-led by their passion, rage, and conviction. They share an ideal or purpose that gives them a group identity and which compels them to act. . . . People who are deeply connected to a cause don't need directives, rewards, or leaders to tell them what to do" (181). Further, "Over time, a network is fueled more by passion than by information. Networks begin with the circulation of information. This is how members find each other, learn from each other, and develop strategies and actions. . . . The essential structure of any network is horizontal, not hierarchical, and ad hoc, not unified" (182).

4. Wheatley, *Leadership and the New Science*, 171.

[As an aside, the interconnectedness of the world order can be understood by watching the reaction of the global markets to the pandemic Coronavirus].

5. Einstein, *The Theory of Relativity*, 66.

6. Omnes, *Quantum Philosophy*, 19.

Omnes went on to explain this derivative notion from Kant: "[A]ll knowledge must go through the mold of our a priori synthetic judgments, the constraints of our mind, so to speak" (219).

7. Malin, *Nature Loves to Hide*, 112.

Capra and Luisi extended this notion:

The 'inner world' of our reflective consciousness emerged in evolution together with the evolution of language and of organized social relations. This means that human consciousness is inextricably linked to language and to our social world of interpersonal relationships and culture. In other words, our consciousness is not only a biological but also a social phenomenon.

Capra and Luisi, *The Systems View of Life*, 270.

8. Capra, *The Tao of Physics*.

Omnes further noted, "We must be willing to give up almost all our old habits of thought, despite the fact that common sense is so well entrenched in our mind that it is practically impossible to ignore it, even for a moment."

Omnes, *Quantum Philosophy*, 170.

9. Cole, *The Hole in the Universe*, 225.

10. Lipton, *The Biology of Belief*, 71.
11. Lipton, *The Biology of Belief*, xxv.
12. Capra and Luisi, *The Systems View of Life*, 392.
13. St. John, *College Organization and Professional Development*, 143.
14. St. John, *College Organization and Professional Development*, 141.
15. Francis Fukuyama, *The End of History and the Last Man* (New York: The Free Press, 1992), 93.
16. Cole, *The Hole in the Universe*, 212.
17. St. John, *College Organization and Professional Development*, 179.
18. Csikzentmihalyi, *Finding Flow*, 13, 14.
19. Wheatley, *Leadership and the New Science*, 191.

Wheatley concludes, "I crave companions, not competitors. . . . Every moment of this journey requires that we be comfortable with uncertainty and appreciative of chaos" (192 and 193).

20. Malin, *Nature Loves to Hide*, 139.
21. Cole, *The Hole in the Universe*.
    Satinover, *The Quantum Brain*.
    St. John, *College Organization and Professional Development*.
22. Capra, *The Tao of Physics*.
23. Capra, *The Tao of Physics*, 192.
24. Capra, *The Hidden Connections*, 75.
25. John Clarke, *Personalized Learning* (Lanham, MD: Rowman & Littlefield, 2002), 309.
26. Rettig, *Quantum Leaps*, 2002.
27. Jon Meacham, *The Soul of America: The Battle for our Better Angels* (New York: Random House, 2018), 36. Quoting President Woodrow Wilson.
28. Capra, *The Hidden Connections*, 2004.
29. John H. Clarke, "Growing High School Reform: Planting the Seeds of Systemic Change," *NASSP Bulletin* (April 1999), 4.
30. Neumann, "Organizational Structures to Match," 95.
31. William Halal, *The New Management: Bringing Democracy and Markets Inside Organizations* (San Francisco: Berrett-Koehler, 1998), 83.
32. L. Rhodes, "Connecting Leadership and Learning." *In a Planning paper developed for the American Association of School Administrators National Center for Connected Learning*, (April 1997), 15.
33. Fareed Zakaria, *The Future of Freedom: Illiberal Democracy at Home and Abroad* (New York: W. W. Norton & Company, 203), 105.
34. Rettig, *Shared Governance*.

This book provides a much more thorough read of values, principles, and processes of shared governance and democratic institutions. It delineates the history of shared governance in higher education, as well as what it could look like should these institutions adopt and adapt these fundamental and seminal democratic notions. This section of the current chapter is borrowed liberally from *Making Shared Governance Meaningful*.

35. March and Olsen, *Democratic Governance*, 22.

36. Edward Greenberg, *Workplace Democracy: The Political Effects of Participation* (Ithaca, NY: Cornell University Press, 1986), 170.

37. D. Dotlich and P. Cairo, *Unnatural Leadership: Going Against Intuition and Experience to Develop Ten New Leaderships Instincts* (San Francisco: Jossey-Bass, 2002), 162.

"Empowerment in complex organizations, however, is essential; it's impossible to compete and grow if the people who are furthest from the customers are making the decisions. Leaders need to trust that those on the front line are in the best positions to make decisions."

To which Atkinson added, "The management principles of democracy, profit-sharing, and information require a collegial approach to sharing information and decision-making. The conventional top-down flows of information, decision-making authority, and responsibility give way to an environment where the opinion of the knowledge worker is valued, sought out, and considered."

Anthony Atkinson, "The Promise of Employee Involvement," *CMA Magazine* 3 (April 1990), 8.

38. Peter Bachrach and Aryeh Botwinick, *Power and Empowerment: A Radical Theory of Participatory Democracy* (Philadelphia: Temple University Press, 1992), 41.

39. E. Davis, and Russell Lansbury, eds., *Democracy and Control in the Workplace* (Melbourne, Australia: Longman and Cheshire, 1986), 35.

Democracies require diversity of people participating and sharing their opinions, and democratic organizations need flexibility in operationalizing their values. But "participation is not equivalent to democracy."

"Democracy thrives on instruments for creating and maintaining diversity. It profits from public criticism and debate, from conflict over values and rules, and from differences that lead to experimentation with alternative practices and exploration of new visions."

March and Olsen, *Democratic Governance* (New York: The Free Press, 1995), 169.

40. Zinn, *Declarations of Independence*, 211–212.

41. Gary Olson, "Exactly What is 'Shared Governance'?" *The Chronicle of Higher Education,* (July 23, 2009), 2.

42. Association of Governing Boards of Universities and Colleges, "Effective Governing Boards: A Guide for Members of Governing Boards of Independent Colleges and Universities," (Washington, DC, 2014), 5–25.

43. www.aaup.org; www.agb.org; www.acenet.edu

44. Larry Gerber, *The Rise and Decline of Faculty Governance: Professionalization and the Modern American University* (Baltimore, MD: Johns Hopkins University Press, 2014), 2.

45. Rettig, *Shared Governance.*

46. Dolan, *Restructuring Our Schools*, 59.

47. Freire, *Pedagogy of the Oppressed.* Translated by Myra Ramos.

48. Henry Giroux, *Teachers as Intellectuals: Toward a Critical Pedagogy of Learning* (Westport, CT: Bergin & Garvey, 1988).

49. Jeanne Theoharis, 2020. "Rosa Park's Biography: A Resource for Teaching Rosa Parks." (Jeanne Theoharis & The Center for the Humanities, Graduate Center, CUNY, 2020). https://rosaparksbiography.org/bio/highlander-folk-school-and-the-criminalization-of-organizing/

50. Shapell. Thomas Jefferson Quotes. https://www.shapell.org/. 2020.

51. Todd Gitlin, "Varieties of Patriotic Experience," In *The Fight is for Democracy: Winning the War of Ideas in America and the World*, ed. George Packer (New York: HarperCollins, 2003), 118.

Bibliography

Alexander, Stephon. "What This Drawing Taught Me about Four-Dimensional Spacetime." *Nautilus.* March 16, 2017.
Association of Governing Boards of Universities and Colleges. 2014. "Effective Governing Boards: A *Guide for Members of Governing Boards of Independent Colleges and Universities."* Washington, DC, 2014.
Atkinson, Anthony. "The Promise of Employee Involvement." *CMA Magazine* 3 (April 1990): 8.
Bachrach, Peter, and Aryeh Botwinick. *Power and Empowerment: A Radical Theory of Participatory Democracy.* Philadelphia: Temple University Press, 1992.
Beyer, L. "The Value of Critical Perspectives in Teacher Education." *Journal of Teacher Education,* 52(2): (March/April 2001).
Blau, Peter. *The Organization of Academic Work.* New York: Wiley, 1973.
Block, Peter. *Stewardship: Choosing Service over Self-Interest.* San Francisco: Berrett-Koehler, 1996.
Bransford, J., A. Brown, and A. Cocking (Editors). *How People Learn: Brain, Mind, Experience, and School.* Washington, DC: National Academy Press, 1999.
Capra, Fritjof and Pier Luigi Luisi. *The Systems View of Life: A Unifying Vision.* Cambridge, UK: Cambridge University Press, 2014.
Capra, Fritjof. *The Hidden Connections: A Science of Sustainable Living.* New York: Anchor Books, 2004.
Capra, Fritjof. *The Tao of Physics: An Exploration of the Parallels between Modern Physics and Eastern Mysticism.* Boston: Shambhala, 2000.
Capra, Fritjof. *The Web of Life: A New Scientific Understanding of Living Systems.* New York: Anchor Books Doubleday, 1996.
Carroll, Sean B. *The Serengeti Rules.* Princeton, NJ: Princeton University Press, 2016. "The Serengeti Rules." *Nature.* Video of the Public Broadcasting System. Edited by Benedict Jackson. Executive Producer: David Guy Elisco, Jared Lipworth, and

Fred Kaufman. Produced by David Allen and Gaby Bastyra. October 9, 2019. Based on the book by Sean B. Carroll. (2016). *The Serengeti Rules*. Princeton, NJ: Princeton University Press.

Champawat, N. "Sarvepalli Radhakrishnan." In Ian McGreal (Ed.). *Great Thinkers of the Eastern World*. New York: HarperCollins, 1995, 279–283.

Clarke, John H. "Growing High School Reform: Planting the Seeds of Systemic Change," *NASSP Bulletin*, 4, 8, and 9 (April 1999).

Clarke, John. *Personalized Learning*. Lanham, MD: Rowman & Littlefield Education, 2002.

Cole, K. C. *The Hole in the Universe: How Scientists Peered over the Edge of Emptiness and Found Everything*. New York: Harcourt, 2001.

College Board. *Trends in College Pricing*. www.collegeboard.org. 2018.

Comstock, D. "A Method for Critical Research," In E. Bredo and W. Feinberg (Eds.) *Knowledge and Values in Social and Educational Research*. Philadelphia: Temple University Press, 1982.

Covey, Stephen. *The Seven Habits of Highly Effective People*. New York: Fireside of Simon & Schuster, 1990.

Csikzentmihalyi, Mihalyi. *Finding Flow: The Psychology of Engagement with Everyday Life*. New York: Basic Books, 1997.

Csikszentmihalyi, Mihalyi. *Flow: The Psychology of Optimal Experience*. New York: Harper Collins, 1990.

Davis, E., and Russell Lansbury (Eds.). *Democracy and Control in the Workplace*. Melbourne, Australia: Longman and Cheshire, 1986.

Dewey, John. *The Later Works of John Dewey, 1925-1953*, edited by Jo Ann Boydston. Carbondale: Southern Illinois University Press, 1938a.

Dewey, John. *Experience and Education*. New York: Kappa Delta Pi, 1938b.

Docking, Jeffrey. *Crisis in Higher Education: A Plan to Save Small Liberal Arts Colleges in America*. East Lansing, MI: Michigan State University Press, 2015.

Dolan, Patrick. *Restructuring Our Schools: A Primer on Systemic Change*. Kansas City: Systems & Organization, 1994.

Dotlich, D. and P. Cairo. *Unnatural Leadership: Going Against Intuition and Experience to Develop Ten New Leaderships Instincts*. San Francisco: Jossey-Bass, 2002.

Einstein, Albert. *The Theory of Relativity and other Essays*. New York: MJF Publishing, 1950.

Fassel, Diane. "Lives in the Balance: The Challenge of Servant-Leaders in a Workaholic Society." In L. Spears (Ed.). *Insights on Leadership: Service, Stewardship, Spirit, and Servant Leadership*. New York: John Wiley & Sons, 1998, 216–229.

Freire, Paulo. *Pedagogy of the Oppressed*. Translated by Myra Ramos. New York: Continuum International Group, Inc, 1970.

Fukuyama, Francis. *Our Posthuman Future*. New York: Farrar, Straus and Giroux, 2002.

Fukuyama, Francis. *The End of History and the Last Man*. New York: The Free Press, 1992.

Gerber, Larry. *The Rise and Decline of Faculty Governance: Professionalization and the Modern American University.* Baltimore, MD: Johns Hopkins University Press, 2014.

Gilligan, Carol. *In a Different Voice: Psychological Theory and Women's Development.* Cambridge, MA: Harvard University Press, 2003.

Giroux, Henry. *Teachers as Intellectuals: Toward a Critical Pedagogy of Learning.* Westport, CT: Bergin & Garvey, 1988.

Gitlin, Todd. "Varieties of Patriotic Experience," In George Packer (Ed.), *The Fight is for Democracy: Winning the War of Ideas in America and the World.* New York: HarperCollins, 2003.

Goleman, Daniel. "Leadership that gets Results." *Harvard Business Review* 78 (2) (2000), 78–90.

Goswami, Amit. "Creativity and the Quantum: A Unified Theory of Creativity." *Creativity Research Journal* 9 (1) (1996), 47–61.

Green, Reginald. *Practicing the Art of Leadership: A Problem-Based Approach to Implementing the ISLLC Standards.* Upper Saddle River, NJ: Merrill Prentice Hall, 2001.

Greene, Brian. *The Elegant Universe: Superstrings, Hidden Dimensions, and the Quest for the Ultimate Theory.* New York: Vintage Books, 2000.

Greenberg, Edward. *Workplace Democracy: The Political Effects of Participation.* Ithaca, NY: Cornell University Press, 1986.

Gribbon, John. *In Search of the Multiverse: Parallel Worlds, Hidden Dimensions, and the Ultimate Quest for the Frontiers of Reality.* Hoboken, NJ: Wiley & Sons, 2009.

Halal, William. *The New Management: Bringing Democracy and Markets Inside Organizations.* San Francisco: Berrett-Koehler, 1998.

Heckscher, Charles and Anne Donnellon (Eds.). *The Post-Bureaucratic Organization: New Perspectives on Organizational Change.* Thousand Oaks, CA: Sage, 1994.

Heckscher, Charles. "Defining the Post-Bureaucratic Type." In Charles Heckscher and Anne Donnellon (Eds.), *The Post-Bureaucratic Organization: New Perspectives on Organizational Change.* Thousand Oaks, CA: Sage, 1994.

Howell, Elizabeth. "What is the Big Bang Theory?" *Space.com.,* November 7, 2017. www.space.com/25126-big-bang-theory.html.

Hoy, Wayne, and Cecil Miskel. *Educational Administration: Theory, Research, and Practice.* New York: Random House, 1982.

Jaworski, Joseph. *Synchronicity: The Inner Path of Leadership.* San Francisco: Berrett-Koehler, 1996.

Jermier, J. "Critical Perspectives on Organizational Control." *Administrative Science Quarterly* 43, (1998), 235–256.

Kaku, Michio. *Visions: How Science Will Revolutionize the 21st Century.* New York: Bantam Doubleday Dell Publishers, 1997.

Kotter, John. *What Leaders Really Do.* Cambridge, MA: Harvard Business School Press, 1999.

Levin, Yuval. *A Time to Build: From Family and Community to Congress and the Campus, How Recommitting to our Institutions can Revive the American Dream.* New York: Basic Books, 2020.

Lipman-Blumen, Jean. *The Connective Edge: Leading in an Interdependent World.* San Francisco: Jossey-Bass, 1996.
Lipton, Bruce. *The Biology of Belief: Unleashing the Power of Consciousness, Matter & Miracles.* New York: Hay House, 2008.
MacTaggart, Terrence. *Leading Change: How Boards and Presidents Build Exceptional Academic Institutions.* Washington, DC: AGB Press, 2011.
Malin. Shimon. *Nature Loves to Hide: Quantum Physics and the Nature of Reality, A Western Perspective.* Oxford, UK: Oxford University Press, 2001.
March, James, and Johan Olsen. *Democratic Governance.* New York: The Free Press, 1995.
Marion, Russ. *Leadership in Education: Organizational Theory for the Practitioner.* Upper Saddle River, NJ: Merrill Prentice Hall, 2002.
Maslow, Abraham. *Religions, Values, and Peak Experiences.* New York: Penguin, 1970.
McLeod, Saul. "Maslow's Hierarchy of Needs." *Simply Psychology (March 20, 2020),* https//:www.simplypsychology.org/maslow.html.
Meacham, Jon. *The Soul of America: The Battle for our Better Angels.* New York: Random House, 2018.
Mursell, James. *Principles of Democratic Education.* New York: Norton, 1955.
Neary, Lynn. "Morning Edition: Interview on Book Publishing." *National Public Radio.* (November 26, 2019).
Nield, David. "Scientists have Demonstrated Quantum Entanglement on a Tiny Satellite Orbiting Earth," *Science Alert* (June 28, 2020).
Neumann, Francis., Jr. "Organizational Structures to Match the New Information-Rich Environments: Lessons from the Study of Chaos." *Public Productivity and Management Review,* 21 (September 1997).
Nichols, Tom. *The Death of Expertise: The Campaign Against Established Knowledge and Why it Matters.* New York: Oxford University Press, 2017.
Niebuhr, Reinhold. *Reinhold Niebuhr: Major Works on Religion and Politics,* Edited by Elisabeth Sifton. New York: Library of America, 1944.
Nield, David. "Physicists Just Achieved the First-Ever Quantum Teleportation Between Computer Chips." *Science Alert* (December 31, 2019).
Olson, Gary. "Exactly What is 'Shared Governance'?" *The Chronicle of Higher Education* (July 23, 2009).
Omnes, Roland. *Quantum Philosophy: Understanding and Interpreting Contemporary Science.* Princeton, NJ: Princeton University Press, 1999.
Owens, Robert. *Organizational Behavior in Education: Adaptive Leadership and School Reform.* New York: Pearson Allyn & Bacon, 2004.
Overbye, Dennis. *The New York Times.* "Infinite Visions Were Hiding in the First Black Hole Image's Rings." (March 28, 2020).
Packer, George (Ed.). *The Fight is for Democracy: Winning the War of Ideas in America and the World.* New York: HarperCollins, 2003.
Penrose, Roger. *The Large, the Small, and the Human Mind.* Cambridge, UK: Cambridge University Press, 1997.
Pine, Ronald. *Science and the Human Prospect.* Belmont, CA: Wadsworth, 2000.

Prigogine, Ilya, and Isabelle Stengers. *Order out of Chaos.* New York: Bantam Books, 1984.
Rettig, Perry. *Shared Governance: A More Meaningful Approach in Higher Education.* Lanham, MD: Rowman & Littlefield, 2020.
Rettig, Perry. "Shared Governance: The 'Keystone' Process to the Higher Education Ecology Survival." *Academy for Advancing Leadership,* (December 2019).
Rettig, Perry. *Reframing Decision Making in Education: Democratic Empowerment of Teachers and Parents.* Lanham, MD: Rowman & Littlefield, 2016.
Rettig, Perry. *Quantum Leaps in School Leadership.* Lanham, MD: Rowman & Littlefield, 2002.
Rhodes, L. "Connecting Leadership and Learning." In a Planning paper developed for the *American Association of School Administrators National Center for Connected Learning,* (April 1997).
Rovelli, Carlo. "Black Hole Evolution Traced Out with Loop Quantum Gravity." *Physics* (11) 127, *American Physical Society* (December 10, 2018).
Satinover, Jeffrey. *The Quantum Brain: The Search for Freedom and the Next Generation of Man.* New York: John Wiley & Sons, 2002.
Senge, Peter. *The Fifth Discipline: The Art and Practice of the Learning Organization.* New York: Doubleday/Currency, 1990.
Sergiovanni, Thomas. *Value-Added Leadership: How to get Extraordinary Performance in Schools.* New York: Harcourt Brace Jovanovich Publishers, 1990.
Sergiovanni, Thomas and Robert Starratt. *Supervision: A Redefinition.* New York: McGraw-Hill, 1993.
Shapell. Thomas Jefferson Quotes, 2020. https://www.shapell.org/
Shlain, Leonard. *The Alphabet Versus the Goddess: The Conflict between Word and Image.* New York: Penguin Putnam, 1998.
Siegel, Ethan. "Ask Ethan: Does a Time-Stopping Paradox Prevent Black Holes from Growing?" *Science,* (January 11, 2020).
Stapp, Henry. *Mind, Matter, and Quantum Mechanics.* New York: Springer-Verlag, 1993.
Starr, Michelle. "A Strange Black Hole is Shooting Out Wobbly Jets Because It's Dragging Spacetime." *Space* (January 1, 2020).
St. John, Edward. *College Organization and Professional Development: Integrating Moral Reasoning and Reflective Practice.* New York: Routledge, 2009.
Talbot, Michael. *The Holographic Universe: The Revolutionary Theory of Reality.* New York: Harper Collins, 2011.
Taubes, Gary. "Schizophrenic Atom Doubles as Schrodinger's Cat—or Kitten." *Science* (May 1996).
Theoharis, Jeanne. "Rosa Park's Biography: A Resource for Teaching Rosa Parks." Jeanne Theoharis & The Center for the Humanities, Graduate Center, CUNY, 2020. https://rosaparksbiography.org/bio/highlander-folk-school-and-the-criminalization-of-organizing/
Voronov, Maxim and Peter T. Coleman. "Beyond the Ivory Towers: Organizational Power Practices and a 'Practical' Critical Post-modernism." *The Journal of Applied Behavioral Science* 39(2) (June 2003).

Waldrop, Michael. *Complexity: The Emerging Science at the Edge of Order and Chaos*. New York: Simon & Schuster, 1992.
Wheatley, Margaret. *Leadership and the New Science: Learning about Organizations from an Orderly Universe*. San Francisco: Berrett-Koehler, 2000.
WICHE: Western Interstate Commission for Higher Education. *Knocking at the College Door*, 2016.
Wolchover, Natalie. "Physicists Debate Hawking's Idea that the Universe had No Beginning." *Quanta Magazine* (June 6, 2019).
Yam, Philip. "Bringing Schrodinger's Cat to Life." *Scientific American*, 124–129, (June 1997).
Zakaria, Fareed. *The Future of Freedom: Illiberal Democracy at Home and Abroad*. New York: W. W. Norton & Company, 2003.
Zemsky, Robert, Susan Shaman, and Susan Campbell Baldridge. *The College Stress Test: Tracking Institutional Futures Across a Crowded Market*. Baltimore, MD: Johns Hopkins University Press, 2020.
Zinn, Howard. *Declarations of Independence: Cross-Examining American Ideology*. New York: Harper Collins, 1990.
Zukav, Gary. *The Dancing Wu Li Masters: An Overview of the New Physics*. New York: Bantam, 1980.

About the Author

Perry R. Rettig, PhD, has been an educator for thirty-eight years with a breadth of leadership experiences. He has written extensively on the topic of leadership and has presented his thoughts to dozens of national and international audiences. *The Quantum University* is his sixth book with Rowman & Littlefield. It examines the newer sciences and how they should impact our leadership and our organizational models. He begins by describing the classical sciences and their impact on present structures. He then describes newer lessons from the sciences and how they should impact the work of educational leaders.

After a dozen years as a teacher and as a school principal in K–12 public schools, Rettig became a professor of educational leadership and administration. The past twenty-seven years have found him in higher education serving in various capacities as a faculty member, associate vice chancellor, vice president for academic affairs, and, most recently as vice president for enrollment management. He has served as a leadership fellow, and as interim deans in the school of education and the school of nursing & health sciences. Presently, Dr. Rettig serves as the Vice President for Enrollment Management and Vice President for the Athens Campus at Piedmont College in Georgia where he continues to maintain his faculty credentials.

www.ingramcontent.com/pod-product-compliance
Lightning Source LLC
Chambersburg PA
CBHW020748230426
43665CB00009B/539